PET PORTRAIT EMBROIDERY

lovingly stitch your dog or cat

A MODERN GUIDE TO THREAD PAINTING

Michelle Staub OF STITCHING SABBATICAL

Photo by
Tristan Gallagher

stashBOOKS®

an imprint of C&T Publishing

PUBLISHER: Amy Barrett-Daffin

CREATIVE DIRECTOR: Gailen Runge

ACQUISITIONS EDITOR: Roxane Cerda

MANAGING EDITOR: Liz Aneloski

EDITOR: Kathryn Patterson

TECHNICAL EDITOR: Debbie Rodgers

COVER/BOOK DESIGNER: April Mostek

PRODUCTION COORDINATOR: Zinnia Heinzmann

PRODUCTION EDITOR: Jennifer Warren

ILLUSTRATOR: Kirstie L. Pettersen

PHOTOGRAPHY COORDINATOR: Lauren Herberg

PHOTOGRAPHY ASSISTANT: Gabriel Martinez

COVER PHOTOGRAPHY by Michelle Staub

PHOTOGRAPHY by Michelle Staub, unless otherwise noted

Published by Stash Books, an imprint of C&T Publishing, Inc., P.O. Box 1456, Lafayette, CA 94549

Library of Congress Cataloging-in-Publication Data

Names: Staub, Michelle, 1992- author.

Title: Pet portrait embroidery : lovingly stitch your dog or cat; a modern guide to thread painting / Michelle Staub of Stitching Sabbatical.

Description: Lafayette : Stash Books, 2021.

Identifiers: LCCN 2021020777 | ISBN 9781644030141 (trade paperback) | ISBN 9781644030158 (ebook)

Subjects: LCSH: Embroidery--Patterns. | Cats in art. | Dogs in art. | Decoration and ornament--Animal forms.

Classification: LCC TT773 .S725 2021 | DDC 746.44--dc23

LC record available at https://lccn.loc.gov/2021020777

Printed in the USA

10 9 8 7 6 5 4

ACKNOWLEDGMENTS

This book would not have been possible without those who let me use their pets and photos as references to create its patterns. A huge thank-you to Alisa, Andrea, Breanne, Daniella, Dayana, Evy, Henry, Jennie, Jessie, Kelly, Roxanne, Sarah, Vibeke, Zyless, Massimo, and The SPCA for Monterey County!

Thanks to C&T Publishing for helping turn my dream book into a reality and for being so wonderful to work with.

Even more gratitude goes to my family and my husband. The process of writing this book, and also my entire embroidery career, has been a lot. Thank you all so much for believing in me and giving me your constant and undying support.

My pets, as always, were a major source of inspiration as I worked on each portrait in this book (you'll see them throughout these pages). I know they can't read, but I'm thankful to them for keeping me warm and entertained during the late nights while I was working.

I also need to thank the wonderful embroidery community I've found across social media. All the people I've met there are so friendly and helpful and are always good for a laugh or for advice—especially my best embroidery friend Paulo Rezende!

Photo by
Tristan Gallagher

CONTENTS

OUTLINED PORTRAITS 20

LAB

22

FRENCHIE

24

YORKIE

26

POODLE

28

SHORT-FUR CAT

30

TABBY

32

LONG-FUR CAT

34

SPHYNX

36

DETAILED PORTRAITS

BLACK LAB
Balto

WHITE CAT
Háma

DALMATIAN
River

SIAMESE CAT
Cookie

PUG
Lilly

BRITISH SHORTHAIR
Cassie

ORANGE CAT
Jasper

GOLDEN RETRIEVER
Guinness

CORGI
Kenzie

TABBY CAT
Pepper

MALTESE MIX
Forrest

POODLE MIX
Jude

INTRODUCTION

My stitching sabbatical started in 2014 during the summer months. Feeling uninspired and suffocated at the idea of starting a career after college, I decided to buy myself some time before I had to get a job by taking up embroidery and attempting to sell my creations online.

One day, on a whim, I decided to embroider my favorite photo of my cat, Purrl. I fell instantly in love with the process and became captivated. Embroidery was unlike any other form of art I had tried, which is saying a lot since I was an art major and dabbled in everything from ceramics to oil painting! Since my first embroidery in 2014 I have worked endlessly to hone my skills. This is something that comes from practice—of which I've had a lot!

While my first pet portrait wasn't perfect, I was proud of what I'd made and quickly started focusing my attention on stitching portraits for other people. I found it so rewarding to create a truly unique piece of artwork to commemorate a pet and celebrate its life, especially when people trusted in me to create a memorial piece.

When I hold a completed portrait in my hands, knowing that I've captured the subject's essence as perfectly as I can—that the pet's owner will love the piece even more than I loved creating it—I realize that this is the ideal artistic outlet for me.

While I've always loved creating things with my hands, embroidery has been the only thing I've stuck with. For me, it's an incredibly gratifying endeavor. Each stitch is consciously and intentionally placed. It's a slow and meditative process that ends up doing wonders for my mental health. Being able to hold and touch my finished pieces and know that I made something from nothing is so rewarding.

I wanted to create a modern thread-painting book that is a little looser with the rules than others you might read. This book is what I wish I had when I first started making embroidered pet portraits. I hope it will cause you to fall in love with embroidery just as much as I have.

HOW TO USE THIS BOOK

Thread painting is the perfect medium for pet portraits. The small stitches look so similar to fur and create a texture like no other medium. You can run your fingers across it and follow the fur and stitch patterns, feeling the texture of the thread. It's almost as if you're touching the pet itself.

This book will teach you how to create your own custom embroidered pet portraits and provide patterns to follow along with. You can embroider the patterns as they are, or you can edit them to make them look like a dog or cat you know.

Each pattern will provide a different fur color palette that can be mixed and matched to create custom palettes. You can also use the patterns as templates to draw your own pets with their own unique fur markings. There are a lot of colors needed for each portrait, and sometimes you may only use one or two stitches of a color. As you buy the colors needed for these projects, however, you'll build a collection of thread to use for future portraits.

There are also additional patterns for floral accents that you can add to your pieces, as well as two alphabets, so you can truly customize your pet portrait with a name or a significant date.

The patterns in this book are very meticulous and require a lot of small stitches. Please make sure you are in a comfortable position for embroidery so you don't strain your eyes or hands. It's okay to take breaks if you feel overwhelmed! The patterns in this book can be followed by both those who are new to embroidery as well are those who already know their way around the hoop.

Try not to compare your work to others. Just take your time and enjoy the process of creating an embroidery. The more you work at it the better you'll get. Enjoy stitching through these patterns and creating your own embroidered pet portraits!

SUPPLIES

FABRIC

There really is no right or wrong type of fabric to use, but you should choose a fabric that is not too thin, transparent, or stretchy. Choose a medium-weight fabric that is sturdy enough to withstand the heavy amount of stitches you'll be making. In addition, you should choose a fabric that has a tight, even weave to it so you can make small and delicate stitches. All of the embroideries in this book are stitched on either cotton twill or Kona Cotton (by Robert Kaufman Fabrics). Linen and calico are also common fabrics to use. I recommend washing your fabric beforehand if you are planning on creating your embroidery on an object that you will occasionally be washing. I also recommend cutting your fabric a minimum of 2″ larger than the hoop diameter. The patterns in this book are designed for a 6″ hoop, so start with a square of fabric at least 8″ × 8″.

Photo by Tristan Gallagher

HOOPS

There are many different types of embroidery hoops, but the most common ones are made from wood or plastic and have a metal screw closure at the top. Sizes range from 3″ to larger than 14″ (8 to 36cm)! The embroideries in this book are made to fit a 6″ (15 cm) embroidery hoop and all embroideries are stitched in Frank A. Edmunds hoops.

The embroidery hoop consists of two parts: the outer hoop and the inner hoop. The fabric goes in between the two, and the screw at the top tightens the outer hoop to keep the fabric taut. You will want to use an embroidery hoop that will keep your fabric drum tight as you work.

tip **It's normal to have to readjust the tightness of your fabric as you work, but if your hoop can't keep your fabric taut at all, you might try using two layers of fabric or wrapping the inner hoop with bias tape. This will give the hoop something to grip.**

NEEDLES

There are a lot of different brands, styles, and sizes of needles. In my experience, needle type doesn't matter as long as you're comfortable working with it. I only use about two or three needles for all of my embroidery. I use a size 10 John James Sharps needle for all of my single-strand embroidery work and about a size 5 needle when working with multiple threads. I recommend buying a multipack containing a variety of needle sizes to get started. A needle threader is a helpful tool to get the thread through the eye if you are having trouble threading your needle.

THREAD

The terms *embroidery thread* and *embroidery floss* can be used interchangeably. In this book I will be referring to it as *thread*. DMC, Anchor, and COSMO embroidery thread are the most common brands on the market.

Hand embroidery thread comes as a skein, and each skein is made up of six individual strands of thread that can be separated. For the pet portraits in this book, you will exclusively be using a single strand of thread to create the fur.

The patterns primarily use DMC thread, and the numbers in the patterns correspond to DMC thread colors. There are number and color conversion charts available that approximate DMC colors (see Supplies and Resources, page 141). However, if you use other brands of thread, the patterns will not look the same when you've finished them. There are a few patterns that use a color from Classic Colorworks or black and white sewing thread from Gütermann.

SCISSORS

It is best to have a large, sharp pair of scissors for cutting your fabric and a second pair of smaller scissors for trimming your embroidery thread. The most common embroidery scissors are the classic stork scissors, but any type of small scissors with sharp, pointed blades will work just as well.

ADDITIONAL MATERIALS

Some additional materials you might find handy include the following:

- An embroidery stand to hold your embroidery so you are free to work with both hands

- Bobbins to wind thread around and organizer boxes to sort and store them

- An overhead light with a magnifying lens so you can work on smaller detailed sections without straining your eyes

- Thread conditioner for outlined portraits or lettering

- Dritz Fray Check or painter's tape to secure fabric edges if you are having issues with the edges fraying while you work

- Pinking shears to trim fabric

REFERENCE PHOTOS

No matter what kind of portrait you're creating, the best portrait of your pet all starts with getting the best possible reference photo.

TIPS FOR TAKING REFERENCE PHOTOS

Lighting

Lighting can make or break a photo: You can't stitch what you can't see! You'll want to take the photo with a moderate amount of natural lighting. Taking the photo in bright sunlight creates harsh shadows and overexposes the fur color. Poorly lit rooms and artificial lighting can hide details and affect the fur coloration.

BAD

GOOD

Angles

Consider the portrait you'd like to stitch. Do you want to embroider a profile? A three-quarter view? You'll want to see your pet's full face. Avoid taking photos of their face hidden by a blanket or resting on the floor. Make sure you can see both of their ears, too!

tip **Take photos at the pet's eye level for best results.**

Expressions

Consider the facial expression—this includes the ears! You want to capture your pet's likeness and their spirit. Capture your dog's perky ears to show their happy personality instead of choosing a photo with folded-back ears that signify nervousness.

BAD

GOOD

Fur

Also consider the color of your pet's fur. You may want to take a photo of black fur in natural daylight to best accentuate the highlights and shadows on your pet's face.

The most important thing is to choose a photo that best represents the pet's spirit, even if you're only able to use older photos as references.

tip **Regularly groomed pets need extra thought. Choose a photo that captures them at their best. Use a photo showcasing your pup's big, floofy curls instead of one from right after her summer cut if that's how you picture her!**

BAD

Photos by Jessica Young

GOOD

TRANSFERRING PATTERNS

The patterns in this book have a lot of details and require precise lines. There are several methods to transferring a pattern. Here are just some of the common ones.

Photo by
Tristan Gallagher

PENCILS, PENS, OR MARKERS

You can use a normal writing tool like a sharp pencil to transfer your pattern. Tape your pattern to a bright window or lightbox and tape your fabric over it. Make your lines precise because the markings will be permanent unless you wash them out with special fabric-stain remover.

Water-Soluble Fabric Pens

These are common and easy to find at most craft stores. Simply wash your fabric and the markings will disappear. Make sure the fabric is thoroughly washed and rinsed or the lines can return.

tip **Most water-soluble pens do not have a fine enough tip to get all of the details for these patterns. Be sure to look for a fine-tipped one!**

Heat-Erasable Pens

You can use a heat-erasable FriXion pen (by Pilot) to trace out your pattern, and the markings will easily disappear with heat from an iron or a hair dryer. *Mark lightly or faint lines will be left behind.* These markings will also reappear in freezing temperatures and can leave bleach marks on denim or dark fabrics. I recommend using the .5mm extra–fine-tipped ones.

FABRIC STABILIZER

An easy way to transfer your pattern is by using a water-soluble fabric stabilizer. A common brand is Sulky Fabri-Solvy Stabilizer. You can either draw your pattern on the stabilizer or print your pattern on it if you've drawn it digitally. Once you're finished stitching, thoroughly soak the embroidery in water and the stabilizer dissolves. This works well for outlined portraits but can be hard to work with when you are doing dense layers of stitches like with detailed portraits (especially if you use a sticky stabilizer).

PRINTING

The most accurate way to transfer your pattern if you've done it digitally is to print it directly onto your fabric. My favorite way is to use a sheet of sticker or label paper and adhere my fabric to it. Trim the extra fabric to the edge of the paper and then send it through your printer. Then you can peel the sticker-paper backing off and see your pattern on the fabric! If you're using an inkjet printer, you can iron the fabric to set the color. The markings can be rubbed away if you handle it a lot, so be careful while you're stitching.

These options may not work for you if you are using a dark-colored fabric. Try using a fine-tipped chalk pencil or white carbon paper to transfer your designs.

tip **I made a video showing my process of printing on fabric. Scan the QR code to view the video!**

BEGINNER STITCHES

HOOPING

When hooping your fabric, you want to make sure your pattern is evenly stretched in the hoop. Your fabric should be drum tight and your pattern shouldn't be warped or stretched.

tip **Keeping fabric tight in the hoop will help you blend colors smoothly since the fabric won't bunch up.**

STARTING AND ENDING THREADS

When beginning your embroidery, thread your needle and pull your thread through so the tail end is about 50% down the length of your thread. Tie a small knot at the opposite end. As you work, make sure you're holding your needle by the eye so the tail doesn't slip out. Keep the tail end about half of the length of your thread as you work, until there is about an inch or two of thread left. Then you can tie it off. You will also be tying off your thread each time you change a color.

To tie off your thread, bring your needle through to the back of your fabric and run it under a few of your previous stitches. Bring your needle through the loop before pulling it all the way through and securing your thread.

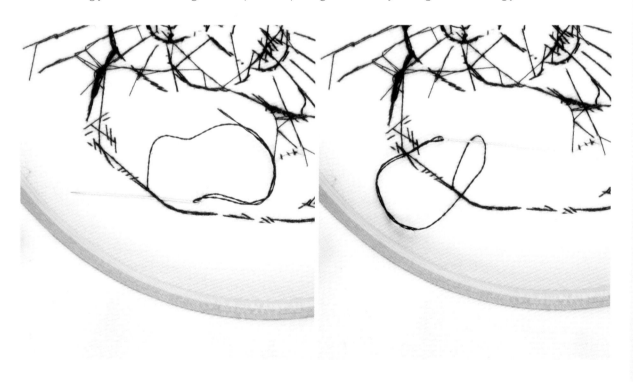

PORTRAIT STITCHES

Backstitch

The backstitch is the backbone for a multitude of stitches. In order to better illustrate the stitches, I am using two strands of thread for these examples; however, you will be using just a single strand as you complete the patterns. Use fine cotton sewing thread like Gütermann to make extra-fine stitches.

For a simple backstitch, bring your needle up at point A, and down at point B. Then start your next stitch at point C and stitch back down into the fabric, meeting point A. Do a series of these to create a row of backstitches.

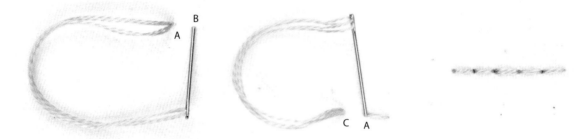

Split Backstitch

Follow the same process as a backstitch for a split backstitch but, instead of bringing your needle down in the fabric at point A, pass your needle through the end of the thread instead. This makes the thread seem connected, and it looks more seamless.

You can also use this technique for a split stitch. Instead of bringing the needle down through the thread of the previous stitch, start your stitch by coming up through the previous stitch.

Outline Stitch

Start your stitch with a backstitch and bring the needle up at C, between points A and B. Instead of pulling the thread all of the way through, leave it loose with the thread curving a bit above your line. Make your second stitch by bringing your needle down and then up at points D and B, respectively—as you move forward in your stitches, the thread will be pulled tighter and create a smooth line. These stitches look thicker in width than split backstitches.

tip **When creating the curved lines of a pet's fur, make smaller stitches as you come around the curve no matter which type of backstitch you are using. The tighter the curve, the smaller the stitches.**

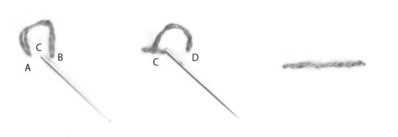

Couching

Sometimes your stitch needs to be moved slightly or have a small bend in it. You can use a technique called *couching* to anchor part of the thread in a new spot. This is useful for lettering or for fixing a stitch that is slightly out of line. Come up through the fabric at the point where you want the thread to bend and use your needle to push your initial stitch to the correct position. Making sure the needle is on the other side of the thread from where you started the couching process, take it back down through the same hole you came up through to finish bending the desired stitch.

CREATING AN OUTLINE PATTERN

DRAWING BY HAND

After choosing the perfect reference photo from which to work, it's time to draw out your design. Draw your pattern freehand if you'd like it to have your own personal style, or trace it directly. I wouldn't recommend using any apps or programs to convert your image into an outline; these never turn out well.

tip **Using tracing paper can make the lines easier to see when tracing it a second time onto the fabric.**

Whether you choose to use a lightbox or a bright window to trace the lines of your pattern, make sure the photo you're using is a size that fits in your hoop. Trace the photo onto a second sheet of paper while holding the photo against your light source. Then use the pattern you drew on the separate paper as your pattern to trace onto the fabric.

DIGITAL DRAWING

Import your photo into your favorite drawing program or app, and lower the photo opacity so you can clearly see where you're marking. Draw your sketch on a separate layer. I like using Adobe Photoshop and my Wacom One tablet to draw my patterns. You can also use a drawing program on an iPad.

Whatever pattern-making method you choose, make sure to capture any of the pet's quirks at this time. Remember, you want your embroidery to look like your pet, not a stock image of someone else's pet!

Use this time to create a road map for your embroidery. Trace out anything that catches your eye, such as changes in fur color or areas of shadows and highlights.

A QUICK NOTE ON ANATOMY

Consider the following when creating a more minimal outlined portrait:

• Do you want lines indicating fur texture to be straight and smooth or scruffy?

• Does the pet have patches of fur that are different colors?

• Is the pet's nose dark colored or lighter toned?

Thinking about these details ahead of time will help you to create a more realistic representation of your pet.

OUTLINED PORTRAITS

WHEN CREATING OUTLINED PORTRAITS, YOU'LL WANT TO BE STITCHING SMOOTH AND PRECISE LINES. I LIKE TO USE A SINGLE STRAND OF DMC THREAD OR A STRAND OF COTTON GÜTERMANN THREAD FOR MY OUTLINES. SOMETIMES BLACK THREAD CAN BE FUZZY. USING A THREAD CONDITIONER WILL SMOOTH IT OUT, GIVING YOU THE BEST RESULTS.

tip **One easy way to separate threads is to trim about an arm's length. While holding the end of the thread with one hand, pull a single strand out from the bunch.**

Here you can see the difference between a single strand of DMC embroidery thread and Gütermann cotton sewing thread.

OUTLINED PORTRAIT PATTERNS

All patterns for these portraits can be found in the back of the book in Patterns (page 134). Full-size downloads of the patterns are also available; see Downloadable Patterns (page 134) for the link. Stitch these patterns using the portrait stitch of your choice. Each pattern has a suggestion of where to start, but since these are outlined portraits you can begin wherever you are comfortable.

You can fill in the eyes with thread or colored pencil to add a pop of color to these portraits.

tip **Using a split backstitch will give you a little more control over the smoothness of your lines.**

Lab

The outline for this pattern is a combination of solid outlines and short stitches for the fur. Use a single strand of DMC thread for the outline and a thin strand of Gütermann thread or sewing thread for the small stitches around the nose and mouth.

Start this pattern on the left ear and work your way clockwise around the pattern. Once you've finished the outer portion, move to working on the facial details. Use a combination of straight lines and small fur lines to indicate darker fur around the nose and eyes and for facial structures like the cheekbones.

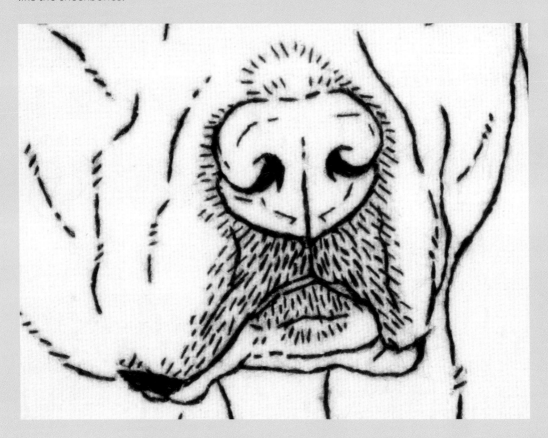

Frenchie

This Frenchie has very short fur, so I used a solid outline for most of the piece. I also added some vines with DMC thread color 522 around the portrait to accent it. Fill in dark areas of the portrait with black thread and leave negative space to create outlines of facial features and pattern markings. This works for pets with black noses or to highlight eyes. Also use this method for outlined portraits of pets with black fur.

I recommend beginning this pattern on the left side of the neck. Work your way around the outer edge of the body before moving to work on the face. You can add some directional lines inside of the nose to accent its unique shape.

Yorkie

It's important not to get lost when creating the pattern for pets with long hair. There should still be a distinguished form under all the fur! I used a strand of Gütermann sewing thread and a stem stitch to create the long, curved pieces of fur. Shorter stitches help to smooth out lines when stitching around a curve.

You may find this pattern easier by starting on the eyes and nose and then following the long fur lines outward. Stitch them one by one, being careful to use small stitches around the curves to make your lines neat and tidy.

Note

This portrait is accented with a bow tie that was made with satin stitches in DMC thread color 927. Satin stitches are just long backstitches placed tightly together to fill in one area of color.

Poodle

Similar to pets with long fur, pets with short fur need some extra thought! Don't get lost in the fur and try to accent every curl. Work in general shapes so you get the idea of the fur without it looking too cluttered. I used a single strand of Gütermann sewing thread and stem stitches for this piece.

Start this pattern by first stitching all of the short fur and facial features and then move on to stitch the long pieces of hair by the ear. Add some small lines in the eye to give more detail.

Short-Fur Cat

Since this cat has shorter fur, I've used mostly solid lines for the portrait outline but have broken up a few sections to indicate some fur texture.

Begin this pattern on the left side of the face and work around the outside. Next, stitch the facial features and ears. Finish the portrait with whiskers.

tip **Sometimes a cat's pupils are round and expressive—you can add extra eye highlights to accent them.**

Tabby

Make sure you're using a fabric that has a tight weave and will allow for a lot of small stitches. Use sewing thread to add thin whiskers and to add varying width to the fur of the stripes.

Start this pattern by stitching the neck fur and chest area. Use lots of small stitches with varying length. Move on to the outside edges of the face, and then stitch the ears and work your way down the portrait from top to bottom. For the darker stripes of fur, first stitch a base layer and then add scattered stitches on top of it to build up the thread.

Long-Fur Cat

Use thicker lines to show areas of the body under the fur. The lines are longer because the fur is longer, but don't make long stitches or your embroidery will look choppy.

Begin this pattern by stitching the fur under the left ear and then work your way clockwise around the inside face portion of the portrait. After filling in the face, stitch the ears and then stitch the long pieces of fur on the outer edge of the pattern. Finish it off by adding whiskers.

Sphynx

Use 1 strand of thread, making thicker stitches around the main outline areas to show variation between the outline and the wrinkles. You want to use solid lines to represent the lack of fur texture. See Patterns (page 134) for the flower crown pattern if you want to add one. Stitch directions for the floral elements can be found in Accenting Pet Portraits (page 126).

Start this pattern by first stitching the ears. Outline the body and wrinkles and then move to the face. No whiskers needed for this one!

Note ————
I used colors 520, 3363, 902, 223, and 24 in the flower crown.

THREAD PAINTING

The most important rule when thread painting animal fur is to not overwork the design while attempting to make the fur look like fur. The thread creates texture, so even an area of solid color has dimension. If you make staggered stitches to make the fur seem "furry," then the portrait could look messy.

There is no perfect formula for stitching pet hair. You could embroider the same pattern several times and each time the stitches would be placed differently. Pet portraits are meant to have dimension and texture to them; the fur is not meant to lie flat and perfectly smooth with all of the stitches placed exactly the same and going in the same direction as if you were stitching a rose petal. Having the stitches flow in an irregular path gives more life to the portrait.

tip **Some thread-painting artists encourage you to stitch with the thread's grain. I find that doing so has no effect when it comes to replicating the texture of fur.**

HOW TO THREAD PAINT

Gradient Blending

Thread painting or needle painting is just a series of irregular long and short stitches. I prefer to do a series of long and short stitches combined with stitches that are even longer and shorter. Your average stitch length should be about the size of a grain of rice, but it's important to let yourself make longer and shorter stitches because doing so will help give texture to your embroidery. Don't make them too uniform, and keep your stitches a bit staggered. Use 1 strand of thread to make your blending look more seamless.

When blending your long and short stitches, it's important to start each stitch by coming up through your previous stitches. If you poke down into them, it creates small needle holes in your thread.

On the subject of holes being left by needles, when thread painting with a single strand of thread it's important to use a size 10 or 11 needle because it's the same width as the thread. If your needle is larger than the width of your thread it will leave holes in your fabric that your thread won't be able to fill.

tip **Sometimes you can't avoid needle holes when working through different areas. Get rid of the holes by using the eye of the needle or your fingernail and gently scratching over the hole to close it.**

If your shape has a clean edge, outline the shape first with a split backstitch with very small stitches. When making your stitches near the edge, bring them down right on the other side of your outline. Here is an example of long and short stitches with contrasting colors.

tip **Use outline stitches along the outer edge of areas such as tongues, noses, and mouths before filling them in to create a crisp border.**

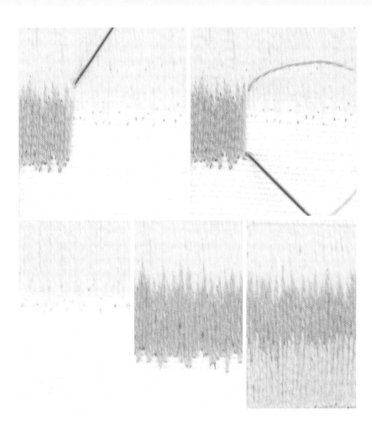

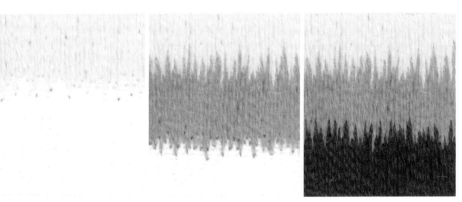

When changing colors, there are 2 ways to blend them together. The first is creating a smooth color gradient. Use 1–3 colors between the ones you want to blend to create a seamless transition.

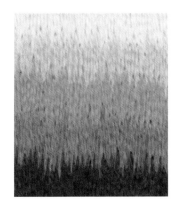

The more colors you use, the more seamless your gradient will look.

Thread Painting Curves and Curls

When thread painting a curved area, make your stitches smaller as you get to the inside of the curve. Stitch over your previous stitches while angling them slightly to fill in a curved shape. It helps to make guidelines to follow and fill in following the curve of the lines.

Top Stitching

Sometimes you will need to create stitches on top of previously stitched areas, like when indicating small hairs near the nose, mouth, or eyes. I will be referring to this as "top stitching." This is the second way to blend thread colors.

Since you can't mix thread colors like you can with paint, sometimes you have to use "top shading" to blend 2 colors together to change the undertone. This tricks the eye into seeing them as being blended together. I will be referring to this as *top blending* or *top shading*, and it is a type of top stitching.

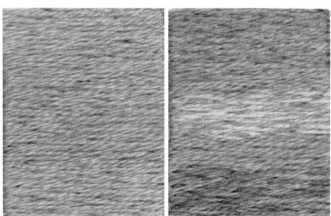

First stitch your area of color, and then stitch a layer of a blending color on top. To make this stitch look neat, make sure all of your stitches are going in the same direction. Top blending is also used to create subtle shading or highlights.

QUICK COLOR CHANGES

Some fur will have abrupt color changes. To blend 2 areas of color so it's not too much of a stark change, first fill in one section of color and then fill in the area around it. Use small top stitches of a third color to blend the 2 colors together. You can then add more top stitches to add subtle highlights or shadows into the fur.

  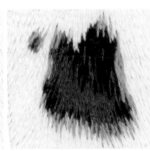 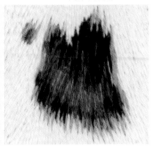

STRIPES AND SPECKLED FUR

Some fur, such as tabby, brindled, and tortoiseshell fur, is full of tiny specks of colors and deep stripes. Not layering the thread properly can make the small hints of color too overwhelming.

For this tabby fur, start by first by using 844 and 646 to create a base layer. Blend the stripe into the fur with 535 and darken the stripe with the color Black Coffee from Classic Colorworks. Create tiny lighter hairs with 648. Make sure your stitches aren't too uniform. These hairs have a high contrast with the color of thread below them, so use 535 between your previous stitches to create the idea of blended fur. Use 3371 to add an even darker color to the stripe to make it stand out. From there, add any other small stitches needed to blend the fur together.

tip **Notice how the fur overlaps the stripe on one side and how the dark fur of the stripe extends over the fur on the opposite side. This shows fur direction.**

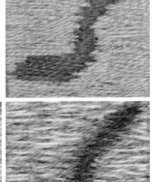 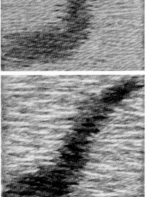

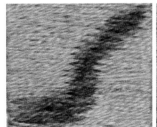 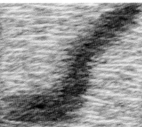

Fur Stitching Order

When thread painting fur, it's not a simple matter of working from the darkest color to the lightest color or stitching all areas of one color first before moving onto the next one. You should work from the background to the foreground.

CHOOSING COLORS

Choosing the correct colors is something that gets easier with practice. You have to train your eye to see colors as thread colors; this comes naturally over time. Specific color palettes will be shown with each portrait, and you can mix and match them to make the patterns look like your own pet. Feel free to use the palettes as is or to add in your own color choices!

When working from your own reference photo, do a bit of editing as needed to make the colors look true to life. There could be things that make sense in the context of the photo but would look strange when stitched in the portrait. Imagine how grass interacts with the pet in a photo, for example. It can reflect green onto a light-colored pet, or bits of it can get stuck in the fur. While realistic, this can be confusing out of context in the embroidered piece.

If you're able to shop for embroidery thread in person, bring your reference photo with you. Hold the thread up to the photo so you can compare colors and make sure you get the right ones!

You can also use cross-stitch pattern generators to help you find colors. It will turn your photo into a cross-stitch pattern with corresponding thread colors. These aren't always 100 percent accurate, but it gives you a place to start and a general idea of what color family to explore.

tip **Choose a color you think you'll need and then choose the corresponding lighter and darker color option. That way if the color you chose originally is wrong, you'll have a backup color to try. A DMC color card is available that is made with real thread organized by color family so you can see the options for their full range of thread.**

Look for undertones in the fur. Is the fur cool toned or warm toned? Are the shadows more blue-gray, neutral, or warm gray? Figuring that out will help your portrait look more realistic and more like the pet you're trying to embroider.

Some colors appear different between the skein and when they are embroidered. If you are unfamiliar with the color palette you're using, do some test blending on a separate piece of fabric before starting on your portrait.

CREATING A PATTERN FOR A DETAILED PORTRAIT

DRAWING THE PATTERN

When you create your pattern, you are also creating a map for your embroidery. For more realistic embroidery, trace the reference photo. You can do this by printing out a photo of the pet, holding it against a bright light, and tracing the pattern out on top of it as you would do with an outlined portrait pattern.

You can also use any drawing program or app such as Photoshop or Procreate: Have your reference photo on one layer and then draw out your pattern on a second layer. I use Adobe Photoshop and my Wacom One tablet to draw my patterns.

Trace out any highlights or shadows, as well as any fur color changes. You want to break down the fur into manageable sections, keeping in mind any limitations of your pattern transfer method. I call these sections my "pattern bubbles," and they create a sort of paint-by-numbers guide to fill in when I go to embroider. I like to make my pattern as clean as possible and not sketchy so I have a clear idea of how to follow it.

tip **Use different colors of pens or pencils when transferring your design to help you differentiate areas of your sketch.**

It helps to have your reference photo on a device where you can zoom in and out and see the details. You can also have printed copies of the photo with different areas magnified if you can't use a device with a zoom feature.

FUR PATHS

Getting the fur paths right is the most important part of creating a realistic portrait. Even if your color choices are a little off, the portrait will still end up looking lifelike because the fur direction looks realistic.

Along with following the fur paths, your stitch lengths should reflect how real fur grows. Fur is shorter closer to the center of the face near the nose and eyes (and on cat ears). As you move outward from the face, down the neck and shoulders, it's naturally longer.

Here are some examples of fur paths. Each detailed portrait pattern in this book is accompanied by a fur-path guide.

tip **Print out a blank copy of your pattern and draw the fur paths on top for easy referencing. Use pencil so you can erase the fur paths if you make a mistake.**

THREAD PAINTING FACIAL FEATURES

There are similarities between stitching cat and dog noses and eyes, but there are differences, too! Usually dogs have larger noses and cats have larger eyes. It's important to stitch what you see in the reference photo, not what you think you know when you imagine your subject. Dogs don't always have visible black pupils and you don't need to have two perfectly symmetrical eye shines.

NOSES

Dog and cat noses can come in many different colors, ranging from black to brown to pink to multicolored.

Follow this formula for filling in the nose:

1 Outline the nose holes with a split stitch and fill them in.

2 Outline the nose with a split stitch as you work through your colors. Fill in the bottom half of the nose with stitches going from the outside to the inside, meeting in the middle.

3 Continue filling in the middle and top area of the nose.

4 Use top stitches to create any highlights.

Dog Noses

Dog noses are big and usually shiny. Use highlights to make them look wet. You can change the look of the nose by either using horizontal or directional stitches.

BROWN NOSE

For a brown dog nose, use 3371, 3858, 779, 09, 3860, and 3861. First fill in the nose and then add any small hairs on top.

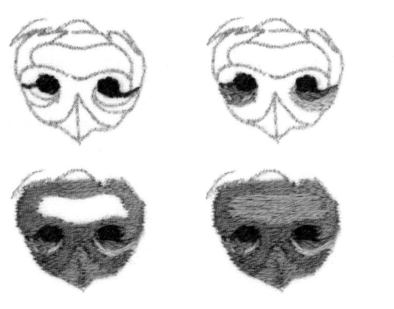
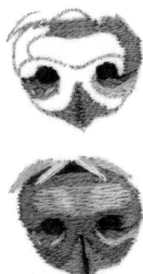

NOSES IN PROFILE VIEW

For a side view of the nose, follow the same formula of stitching the nose mentioned in Noses (page 45). Use 310, 3772, 407, 224, 451, and 3860 to fill in the nose. Add highlights with 819.

SQUISHED NOSE

When making a more curled nose, you can change the direction of the stitches to accent the shape. For this nose, use 310, 3799, 535, 04, and 03. The highlight brings out the stitches as they curve around the nose and draws attention to its overall shape.

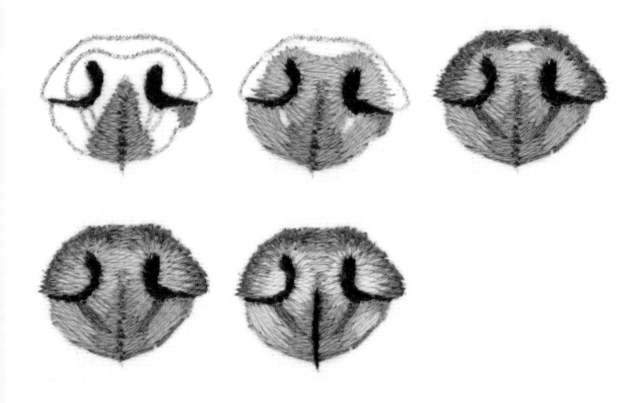

Cat Noses

Cat noses are similar to dog noses but a little more simple. They are not as reflective and there is a smaller area to add color. Use horizontal stitches to fill them in.

ORANGE-AND-PINK NOSE

For this color of nose, use the same process as filling in the dog nose. Use 779, 3859, 632, 3779, and Classic Colorworks' Black Coffee (CCBC) to stitch this nose.

PALE CAT NOSE

Sometimes a cat's nose can appear to be a pale pink. For this nose, I used 3860, 224, and 3774. I added a bit of shadow in the nostrils with CCBC.

EYES

Like noses, eyes come in all sorts of different colors for cats and dogs!

Follow this formula for filling in the eyes:

1 Stitch the pupil of the eye.

2 Fill in the iris.

3 Add any highlights on top if they didn't already get stitched.

4 Outline the eye with a darker thread color and stitch the eyelid around it.

Dog Eyes

Dog eyes are usually smaller than cat eyes in portraits because the dog's face is larger. Layer from the darker color to the highlight.

ROUND EYE

Large round eyes have a lot of room for reflections and color depth in the iris. For this eye, use 310, 801, 938, and 3862. For the eye shine, use 318 and BLANC. For the eyelid, use 310, 535, CCBC, and then highlight with 04 and 03.

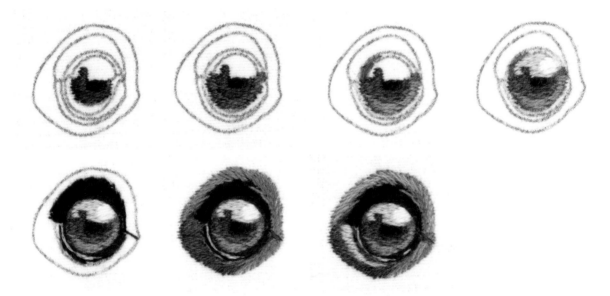

EYES IN PROFILE VIEW

Eyes from the side can be really small, so it's important to capture as many details as you can. Use 310, 938, and 839 to fill in the eye. Add a highlight to the pupil with 535 and add more highlights with BLANC. After stitching the eye, use 535, 779, and 3033 to fill in the fur around the eye and stitch the small eyelashes.

Cat Eyes

The size and shape of the cat's pupil can bring a lot of personality into the portrait. Cat eyes are larger so there is more room for blending and colors. If a pupil is large, then there is a lot of room for reflection. Cat eyes look best when you use horizontal stitches to fill them in. You can create a playful and artistic look by having stitches curve around the eye in a circular pattern or spreading out from the pupil in a starburst.

tip **Use sewing thread to outline the finished eye so the outline of the iris isn't too dark or thick.**

GREEN EYES

Fill in the pupil and the corner of the eye with 310 and 844. Stitch the iris with 3364, 372, 520, and 772. The reflection of the eye is large and reflects the sky; use 931 to fill in half of the highlight and BLANC to fill in the brighter parts. Define the pupil of the eye with 310 and use 535, 3364, and 310 to stitch the eyelid.

BLUE EYES

Sometimes a fully black pupil looks harsh with light blue eyes. Fill in half of the pupil with 823 and half with 310. Leaving space for the highlight, add 3753, 168, 414, 3755, and 3325. Use a few top stitches of 3760 to add more vibrance to the eye. Fill in eye shines with BLANC and add small highlights along the edge with 3752. Outline the eye with 310 for the eyelid.

OTHER FEATURES

Cat Ears

Cat ears can be tricky. They can appear pink in one photo and bright orange in another because of how the light shines through them. It's best to work from the background to the foreground, so stitch the inside of the ear and then the small hairs in front.

After outlining the ear with a split backstitch, fill in the outer ear with BLANC. Fill in the middle portion with 225, 224, 407, 3861, and 3860, making sure to blend the colors into each other. Fill in the bottom left portion of the ear with 3779 and BLANC. Before stitching the ear hairs, fill in the right edge with 225, 224, 407, and 3861. Fill in the ear hair with 01 and BLANC. Finish the ear by stitching hairs in front of it at the base.

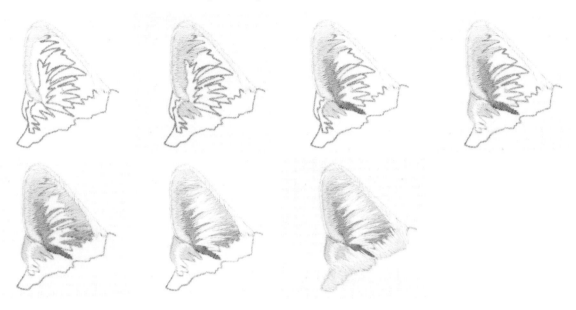

Dog Tongues and Mouths

Dog tongues, gums, and teeth have a surprising number of colors in them. Treat them with the same care you would stitching any other part of the portrait. Tongues can range from a dark pink to a bubblegum pink. Making the tongue and gums too pale can make the dog look sickly.

When stitching teeth, stitch the gums around them first before filling in the teeth. Use a darker gum color to make small stitches between the teeth to define them. For this mouth I used 3858, 3722, 223, and 09 for the gums, and 3866 for the teeth. Add a small highlight on the gums with 778.

When stitching tongues, the stitches can either go horizontally or flow vertically with the movement of the tongue.

tip **Using horizontal stitches in the eyes, nose, and mouth areas helps to separate those areas from the fur.**

For this tongue, I used 3861, 778, 3354, and 963. Use top blending with 316 and 761 to blend areas of the tongue together. I used horizontal stitches for this example, but you can also use vertical ones as seen with this portrait later in the book.

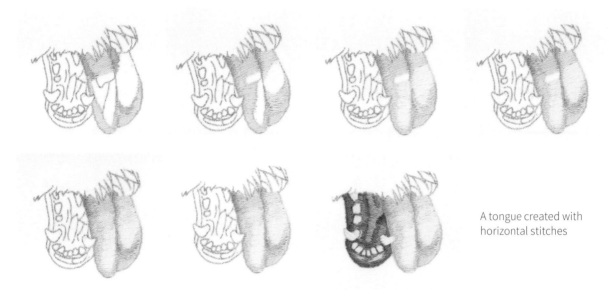

A tongue created with horizontal stitches

Whiskers

Both dogs and cats have whiskers. Some dog portraits have such subtle whiskers that it looks odd to embroider them, so it's okay to leave them out. Cat portraits should always have both forehead and cheek whiskers.

Long whiskers aren't straight; they curve a little. Use short split stitches to create a seamless curve. For short dog whiskers you can use a few top stitches.

tip **You can practice each of these features on a separate hoop.**

Note ————————————————

Senior pet portraits are a bit different from other pet portraits. Consider if their eyes are cloudy and how their fur is a bit unkempt or wrinkly. Their faces may be white with age and have brown tear or saliva stains. Adding these elements can show the age of the pet and will highlight their unique qualities.

ALL PATTERNS FOR THESE PORTRAITS CAN BE FOUND IN THE BACK OF THE BOOK IN PATTERNS (PAGE 134). EACH PROJECT HAS A COLOR GUIDE SHOWING WHICH COLORS ARE USED WITH EACH PATTERN. THE COLOR GUIDE DOES NOT SHOW EVERY STITCH OF COLOR, BUT INSTEAD IT GIVES A GENERAL IDEA OF HOW THE COLORS FILL IN THE PATTERN BUBBLES. NOT EVERY SINGLE COLOR CHANGE HAS BEEN TRACED OUT SO AS NOT TO COMPLICATE THE PATTERN TOO MUCH. DO NOT STITCH THE COLORS ONLY IN THE PATTERN BUBBLES THEMSELVES WHEN CREATING THE FUR. LET THE COLORS FLOW OUT AND BLEND INTO EACH OTHER; OTHERWISE THE PATTERNS WILL LOOK CHOPPY.

There will be a color guide along with a complete list of colors for the portraits before each pattern. As previously stated, all color numbers correspond to DMC thread colors. Some patterns also use a thread color from Classic Colorworks: Black Coffee. This will be referred to as *CCBC* on the charts.

As you work, you will notice things you wish to change or add to a previous area. This is okay and it's fine to bounce around between sections as long as it doesn't interrupt your flow from the background to the foreground of the portrait.

It might be expensive to buy so many thread colors when starting out, but soon you'll have all the thread you need to do any color of pet. Each pattern in this book uses anywhere from 10 to 42 colors, and to stitch every pattern provided you will need 120 colors. Since you are only using a single strand of the skein at a time, the thread you buy to make the patterns in this book will last you through many portraits.

Black Lab | *Balto*

THIS EMBROIDERY ONLY USES TEN COLORS. It's best to blend the thread and create your areas of highlight and shadow by stitching in layers since the color palette is limited. Sometimes black fur will reflect either blue or brown tones, so don't be afraid to add color into your pattern if you are stitching your own pet with black fur. This pattern was stitched on white cotton twill.

Photo by Vibeke Sandvik

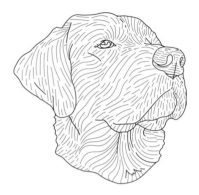

Fur path guide

THREAD COLORS

BLANC	3799	801
03	310	938
04	3863	
535	433	

Color guide

EMBROIDERY

1 Begin your embroidery in the upper right corner of the ear, following the color and stitch guides. Use 310, 3799, 535, 04, and 03.

tip **Keep these stitches shorter, neater, and compact like the short fur on the ear.**

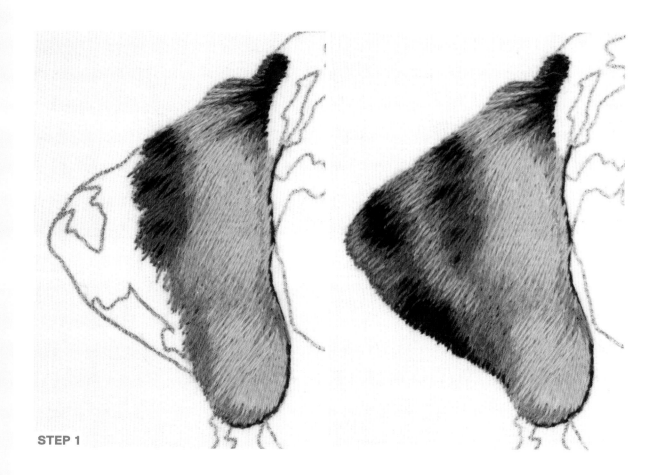

STEP 1

2 Move to the neck next. Use longer stitches to create a furrier and fluffier look. You can either start at the top of the chin and work down or start on the left side and work to the right. Use 310, 3799, 04, and 03. Use top stitching to create the fur highlights.

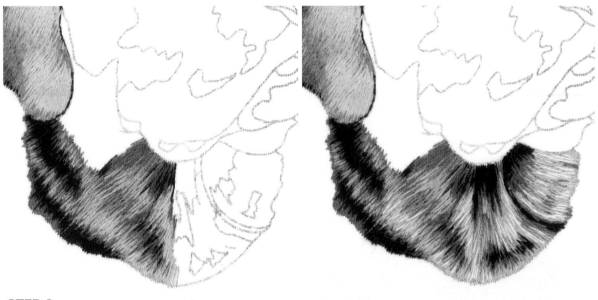

STEP 2

3 Stitch the nose and eye before beginning on the face. Fill in the nose with 310, 3799, 535, 04, and 03. For the eye, use 310, BLANC, 938, 801, 433, and 3863.

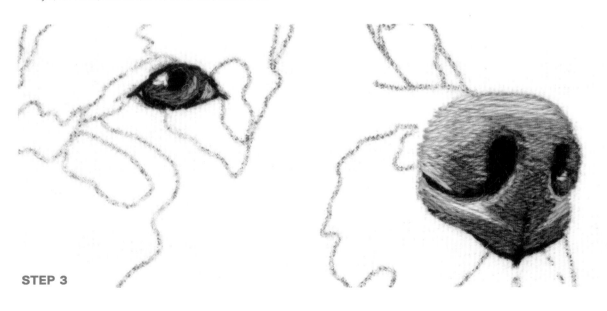

STEP 3

4 Fill in the face by working outward from the nose and using 310, 3799, 535, 04, and 03. Resist the urge to make long stitches here.

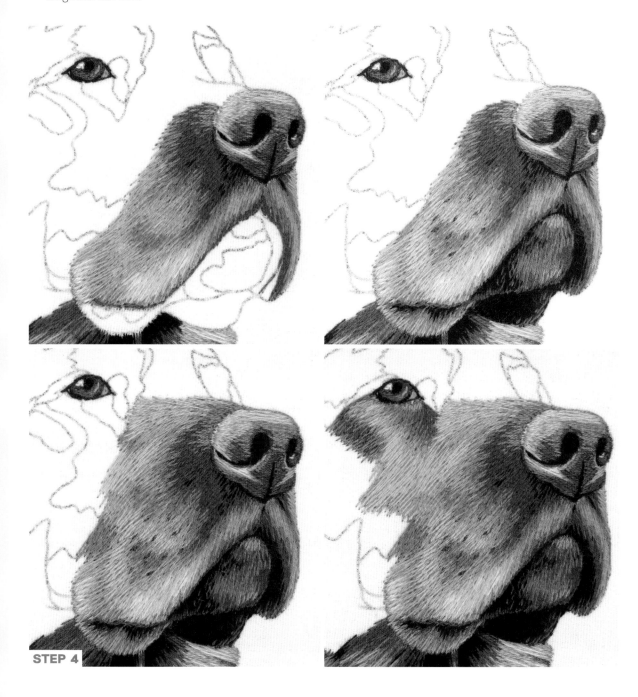

STEP 4

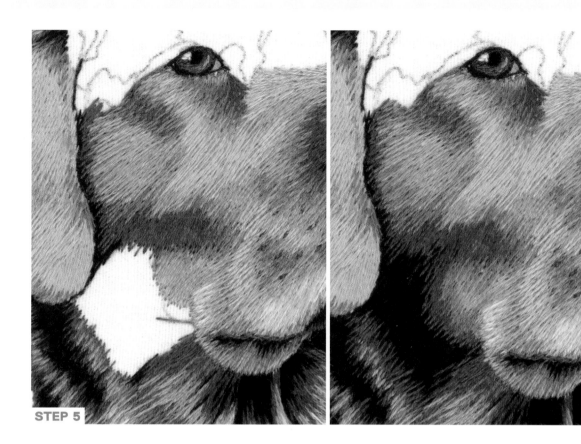

STEP 5

5 Using the same colors as the previous step, continue filling in the face and connect it to the side of the jaw under the ear. Use lots of layers to both blend the colors and create highlights and shadows around the bone structure.

6 Stitch the dark areas around the brow bones to finish the portrait. Use 310, 3799, 535, 04, and 03 in this section. Make small stitches above the brow to create a highlight. Blend the thread until you reach the top of the ear.

STEP 6

White Cat | *Háma*

WHITE FUR ISN'T JUST PURE WHITE AND GRAY— there can be yellow or blue tones to it as well. You can substitute the colors of this pattern with blacks and grays to create an all-black cat. This pattern was stitched on off-white cotton twill.

Fur path guide

tip **If you have a pet with white fur, try stitching the pattern on colored or off-white fabric to make the fur pop. Make sure your stitches are compact so no colored fabric will show through.**

THREAD COLORS

BLANC	370	224
01	3013	407
02	830	452
648	3787	451
844	819	3861
CCBC	3774	3860
310	225	
3047	3779	

Color guide

EMBROIDERY

1 Start your embroidery on the left side of the face. Fill in this section with 01 and 02, and use 648 to add top shading to darken the area next to the cheek. Do the same on the right side of the face with 01 and 648.

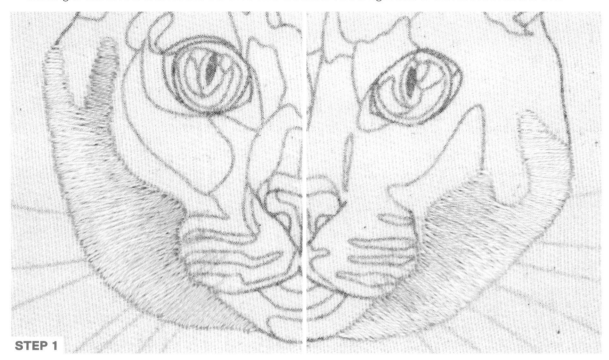

STEP 1

2 Continue stitching the right and left side of the face with BLANC and 01.

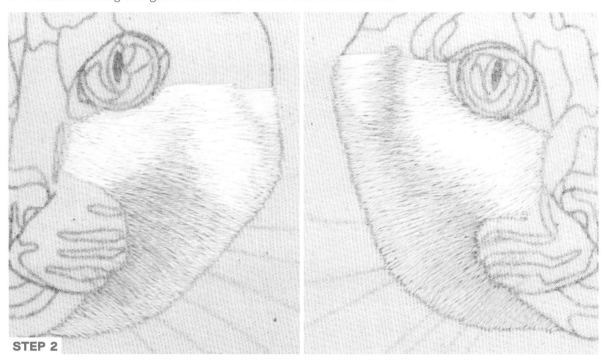

STEP 2

3 Stitch the eyes before continuing to work on the face. Use 543, 451, and 3861 to make the eyelids. Fill in the eyes with 310, 844, 370, 830, 3013, 3047, and 3787.

STEP 3

4 Move on to the chin. Starting at the top of the chin and working your way down, fill it in with 451, 224, 452, 01, 02, and BLANC.

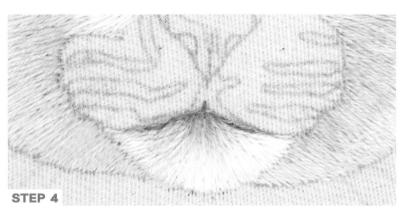

STEP 4

5 Starting at the center and working your way out, stitch each cheek with 01, 02, and BLANC. Top shade with 225 near the centerline between the cheeks. Use 648 to create the indents where the whiskers sprout.

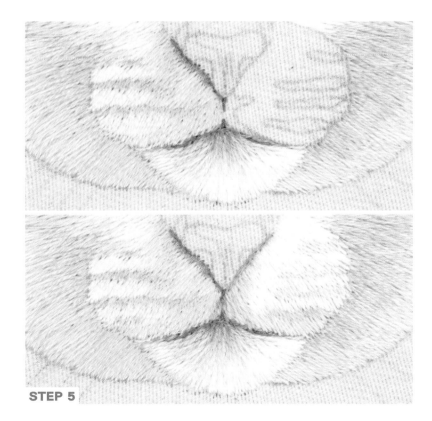

STEP 5

6 Fill in the nose with 3860, 224, 3774, and CCBC. Being sure to follow the stitch guidelines, stitch the bridge of the nose with 01 and BLANC.

tip **For a more in-depth look at the nose and ears, see Thread Painting Facial Features (page 45).**

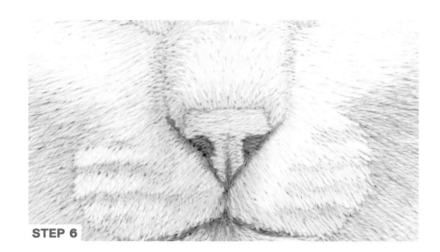
STEP 6

7 Fill in between the eyes and the brow bones. Create a shadow above the left eye by top shading with 648.

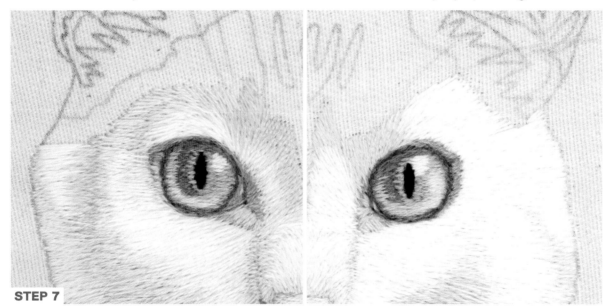
STEP 7

8 Stitch the top of the forehead with BLANC and 01.

STEP 8

9 Before finishing the forehead, fill in the ears. Stitch the inner ears with 225, 224, 407, 3779, and 3861, and then add the ear hairs with 01 and BLANC. Follow the same process for the right ear, adding 819 to the top of the right ear.

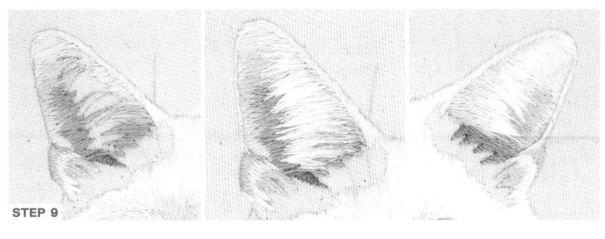

STEP 9

10 Stitch the area of fur in front of the ears with 01, and then add a few hairs with BLANC.

STEP 10

11 Finish the portrait by adding whiskers with a split stitch and BLANC.

STEP 11

Dalmatian | *River*

IT'S IMPORTANT TO THINK ABOUT HOW THE LIGHT REFLECTS OFF THE FUR when creating pets with different areas of fur color. Different colors reflect light in different ways. For example, black fur will be more reflective than white. This pattern uses almost all of the same colors in each step, so while it can be tedious at first, it soon becomes familiar. This pattern was stitched on Kona Cotton in the color Peony.

Photo by Jennie King

Fur path guide

THREAD COLORS

BLANC	3799	801
01	CCBC	938
02	310	3371
03	3861	3820
04	779	3829
535	3862	869

Color guide

EMBROIDERY

1 Begin this portrait by stitching the lower neck area. Work from the left side to the right side. For a guide on how to blend contrasting areas of color, see Quick Color Changes (page 41).

Use 310, 3799, 535, 03, 02, 01, and BLANC for the lower neck.

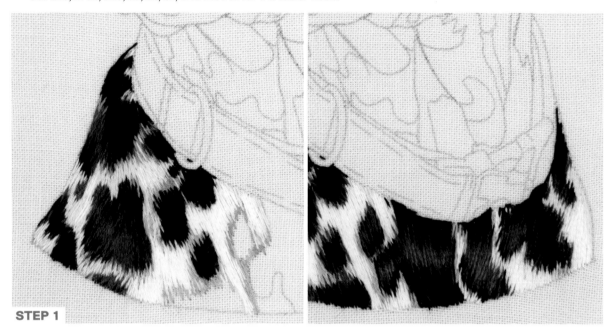

STEP 1

2 Moving up to the collar, first stitch the metal hardware using 3799, 535, 04, 03, and 02. Outline the areas of the hardware with 310. For the yellow collar, use 3829, 3820, and 869.

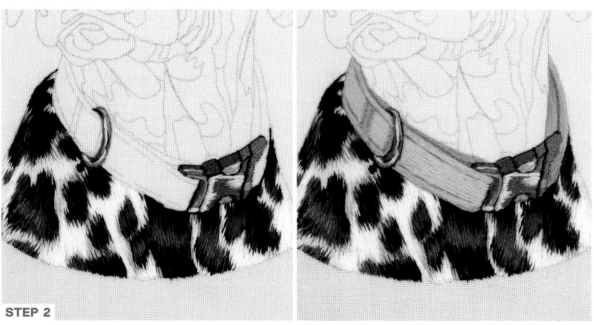

STEP 2

3 Being sure to follow the curve of the fur paths, stitch the upper area of the neck with 310, 3799, 535, 04, 03, 02, 01, and BLANC.

STEP 3

4 Stitch the ears using 310, 3799, 535, 04, 03, 02, 01, and BLANC. Start at the top of the ear near the head and work your way downward toward the tip of the ear.

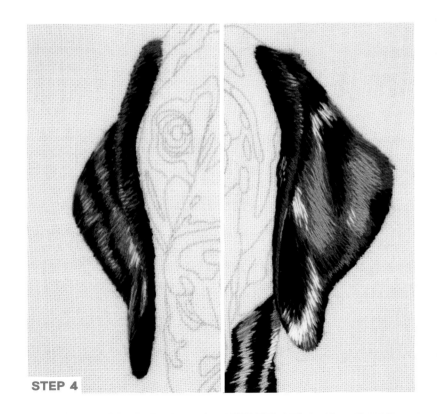

STEP 4

5 Do the nose and eyes before starting on the face. Use 310, CCBC, 3799, 535, 04, and 02 for the nose. To stitch the eyes, use 310, 3371, 938, 801, 01, 3862, and BLANC. Add a few stitches of 3861 in the white part of the eye.

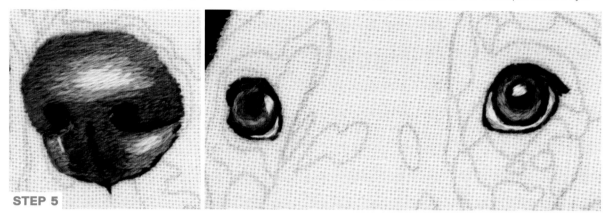

STEP 5

6 Move on to the chin and snout area. For the chin, start at the top and work your way downward with 310, 3799, 535, and 04.

Use 310, 3799, 535, 04, and 01 for the left side of the snout.

For the right side of the snout, use 310, 3799, 535, 04, 03, and BLANC.

Use 779 to stitch the pink tone by the corner of the mouth.

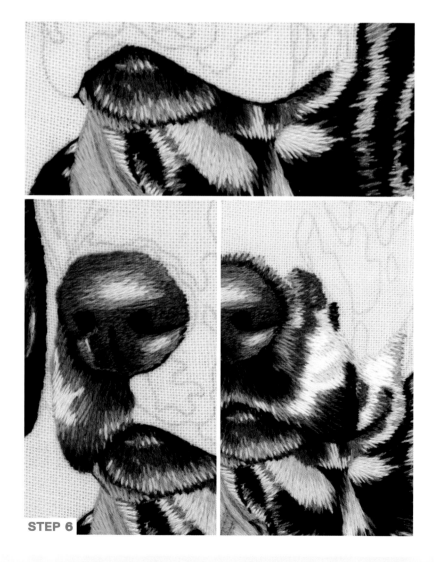

STEP 6

7 Starting around the eye, fill in the left side of the face with 310, 3799, 535, 04, 03, 01, and BLANC.

8 Continue working your way across the face by stitching the area in the middle. Start at the nose and work your way upward. Use 310, 3799, 03, 02, and BLANC here.

9 Fill in the right side of the face, again working from the eye outward. Use 310, 3799, 535, 04, 03, 02, 01, and BLANC in this area. Make sure you add in the tiny white eyelashes!

STEP 7

STEP 8

STEP 9

10 Finish the portrait by stitching some small whiskers with white sewing thread and a split stitch.

STEP 10

Siamese Cat | *Cookie*

THE COLOR BLACK COFFEE FROM CLASSIC COLORWORKS, also known in this book as CCBC, is the perfect shade of deep gray/brown needed to blend the black and brown fur. Siamese cats can have both cool and warm undertones. This cat's cool undertones can be seen in the blue highlights on his face. This pattern was stitched on Kona Cotton in the color Shale.

Photo by Andrea Linda Bruell

Fur path guide

THREAD COLORS

05	3862	779
07	801	844
08	938	762
543	3371	168
842	535	3753
841	413	3752
840	3799	3325
839	CCBC	3755
838	310	414
3864	451	3760
3863	3860	823

Color guide

EMBROIDERY

1 Start the embroidery on the chest. Use 3864, 543, 07, 840, 841, and 842 in this area.

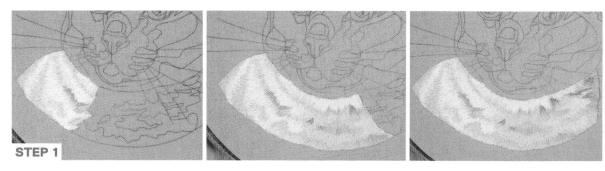

2 Work your way up around the side of the face with 3862, 3863, 3864, 841, 801, 838, 839, and 3371.

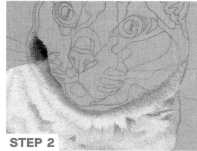

3 Fill in the chin with 779, 3371, 801, and 838. Add a few top stitches with 535 and 451.

4 Fill in the nose with 844, CCBC, and 310.

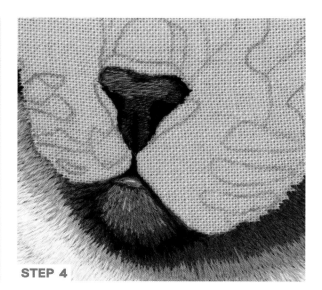

12 Finish filling in the ears with 938, 779, 451, 08, and 3860, and then stitch the inner ear hairs with 3371, CCBC, and 535.

13 Stitch the area of fur in front of the ears with 08, 841, and 840.

14 Finish the portrait by using 842 and a split stitch to stitch the whiskers on the forehead and then using 05 for the whiskers on the face.

Pug | *Lilly*

WRINKLES ARE A GOOD LESSON IN USING SHADOWS and highlights to create depth. Pugs also have large and expressive eyes, which means that you're able to fill them in with a lot of detail. This pattern was stitched on Kona Cotton in the color Peony.

Photo by Kelly West

Fur path guide

THREAD COLORS

BLANC	842	535
3865	3864	3799
3866	841	CCBC
ECRU	840	310
822	839	3861
644	648	318
05	646	3862
06	645	801
07	03	938
08	04	3371

Color guide

EMBROIDERY

1 Starting at the left side of the neck, use 3865, ECRU, 3866, 06, 822, 644, and 05 and work your way to the right side. Use 07, 646, and 645 in the dark area under the chin.

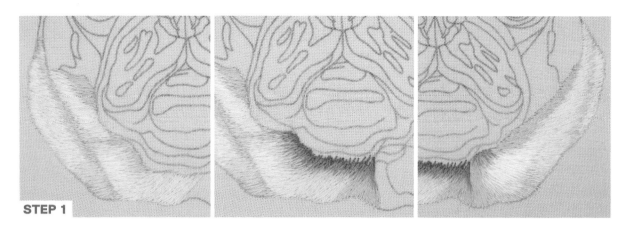

STEP 1

2 Fill in the chin with 310 and CCBC, and add small fur highlights with 535 and 04.

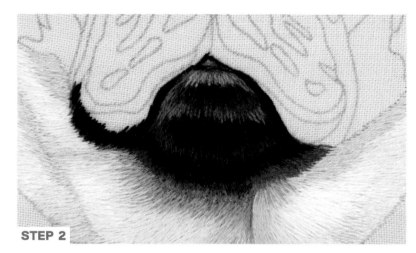

STEP 2

3 Stitch the left cheek and the right cheek using 310, CCBC, and 535. Add top shading with 04 to create highlights.

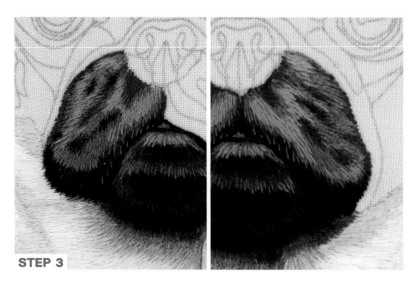

STEP 3

4 Use 310, 3799, 535, 04, and 03 to stitch the nose.

tip **To see a more in-depth look at the pug's nose and eyes, see Thread Painting Facial Features (page 45).**

STEP 4

5 Stitch the top of the nose and the edges of the snout with 07, 08, 842, 535, and 3864. Use small stitches here.

STEP 5

6 Fill in the eyes with 318, 310, BLANC, 938, 3371, 801, and 3862, and make a small stitch of 3861 in the tear duct on the right eye.

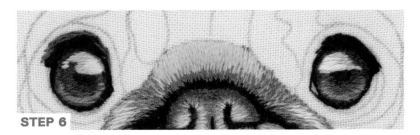

STEP 6

7 Use 535, 310, CCBC, 04, and 03 to stitch the eyelids. Blend the bottom of the eye into the cheek with 3371, 839, 07, and 840. Make the eyebrow with 3371, 839, 310, 07, 06, 08, 842, and 3866.

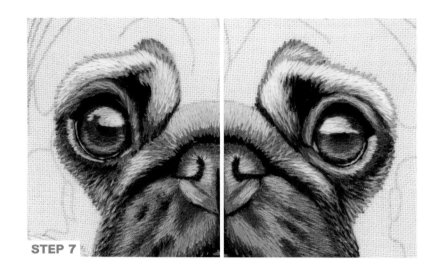

STEP 7

8 Starting near the cheek and working outward, fill in the left cheek first using 841, 06, 05, 842, 3866, and 3865. Make the little whisker spot on the cheek with 04 and 07. Do the same with the right cheek, adding a bit of 648 and 839.

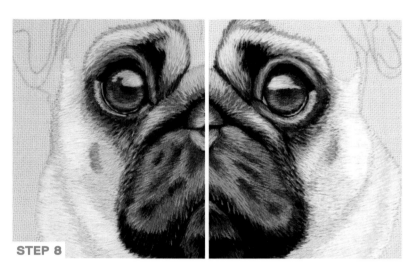

STEP 8

9 Before starting on the forehead, stitch the ears using 310, CCBC, 3799, 535, 04, and 07.

STEP 9

10 Start stitching the wrinkles in the forehead. Stitch the crease first with 07, and then stitch the lighter shadows around the crease with 06 and 842. Add a few stitches of 08 in the creases to darken them. Fill in the fur between the creases with 3866.

STEP 10

11 Continue filling in the center of the forehead with the same colors as the previous step. Start at the bottom near the nose and work your way upward.

12 Stitch the rest of the forehead using the same colors from Steps 10 and 11, working from the center of the forehead out to the ear.

STEP 11

STEP 12

13 Finish the portrait by adding whiskers to the side of the face with 03. Use 04 and 3799 to stitch the small lip hairs and longer cheek whiskers.

STEP 13

British Shorthair | *Cassie*

SOMETIMES THE SHADOWS AND HIGHLIGHTS ON THE FUR ARE VERY SUBTLE. Use a lot of top shading to make the colors blend softly. Cassie is a cat of few colors but makes up for it in the blending and texture of her fur. This pattern was stitched on Kona Cotton in the color Shale.

Photo by Dayana Dancheva

Fur path guide

THREAD COLORS

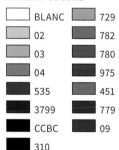

BLANC	729
02	782
03	780
04	975
535	451
3799	779
CCBC	09
310	

Color guide

EMBROIDERY

1 Following the directional lines for the fur, begin this portrait at the bottom. First stitch the dark cracks in the fur and blend them into the rest of the fur. Although you are not stitching tabby fur lines here, the technique is the same as demonstrated in Stripes and Speckled Fur (page 41). Use 3799, CCBC, 535, 04, and 03 in this area. Add a few extra highlights with 02.

STEP 1

2 Continue moving upward toward the chin and the left side of the face. Use 3799, 535, and 04 here.

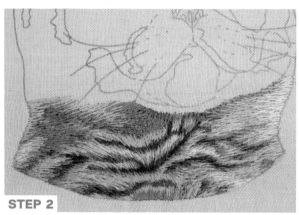 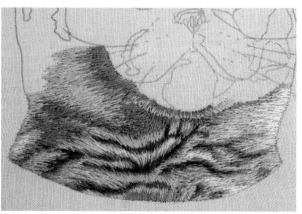

STEP 2

3 Keep filling in the sides of the face, using a lot of top blending with 04 and 03.

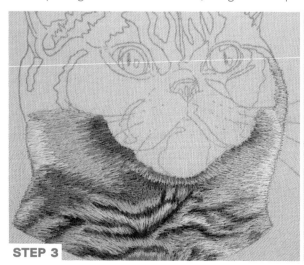 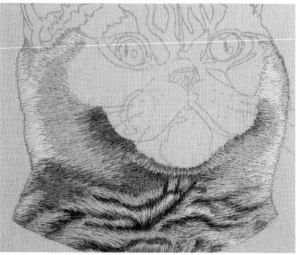

STEP 3

4 Moving to the eyes, fill them in with 310, 729, 782, 780, and BLANC, and use 975 to deepen the outer circle of the eye. You can add small highlights to the pupil with 3799.

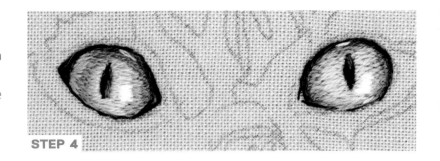

STEP 4

5 Continue filling in the fur on the left side of the face by using a lot of top blending and the colors 535, 04, and 03.

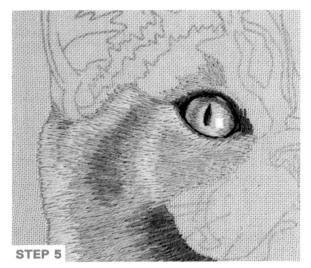

STEP 5

6 Using 310, 3799, and 04, fill in the nose. Stitch the upper area near the eye with 535, 04, 03, and 02.

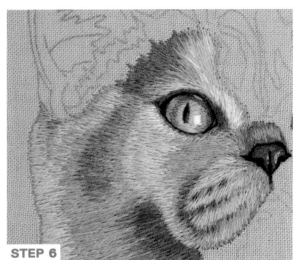

STEP 6

7 Fill in the cheeks and chin with 3799, 535, 04, and 03.

STEP 7

8 Stitch the area under the right eye by using 3799, 535, 04, 03, and 02.

9 For the forehead, use 3799, 535, 04, 03, and 02.

STEP 8

STEP 9

10 Next, fill in the middle of the ears. For the left ear, first use 779 to create a base layer, and then stitch over it with 535 to create an area with a slight undertone. Continue filling in the ear with 09, 535, and 3799.

For the right ear, use 779, 451, 04, and 535. Stitch the outer area of the ear with 535 and 04.

Finish filling in the ears by adding the hairs in the ear with 3799, 535, and 04.

STEP 10

11 Finish the portrait by stitching the areas in front of the ears with 3799, 535, and 04. Stitch the whiskers with 03.

STEP 11

Orange Cat | *Jasper*

WHEN STITCHING ORANGE CATS, there is a very fine line between yellow, orange, and brown. Mixing the colors evenly will create a good overall tone. This pattern was stitched on Kona Cotton in the color Limestone.

Photo by Jessie Gray

Fur path guide

THREAD COLORS

BLANC	801	3032
01	3866	3768
02	3864	844
648	3863	758
310	3862	3064
739	842	3772
738	841	778
437	613	3726
436	07	453
435	3348	452
434	3364	3861
433	3013	

Color guide

EMBROIDERY

1 Start this portrait by stitching the nose with 310, 758, 3064, and 3772.

2 Moving down to the chin, use small stitches to make the mouth with 3726 and 778. Stitch the chin with 3861, 452, 453, BLANC, 648, and 01. Layer the stitches along the side of the chin to blend evenly.

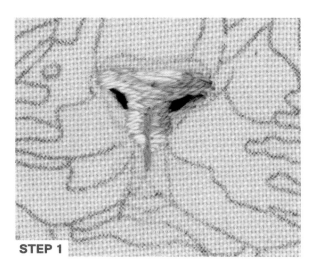

STEP 1

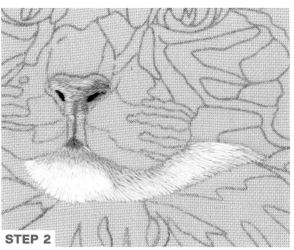

STEP 2

3 Stitch the left cheek with 842, BLANC, 3866, 3863, and 3864. Use 433 for where the whiskers come out. Do the same with the right cheek. Use 453 to highlight the left edge of the nose.

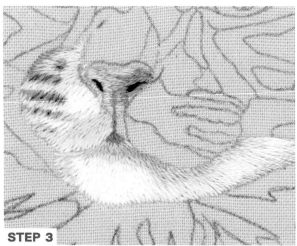

STEP 3

4 Stitch the area next to the left cheek with BLANC and 01. Next, move down to the neck fur. Fill in with 738, 842, 3863, 739, 07, and 648.

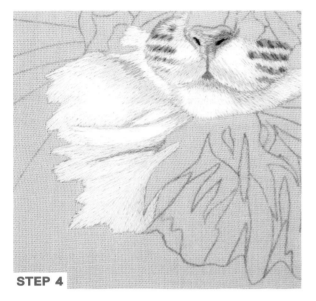

STEP 4

5 Continue filling in the neck fur. Use 3864, 3863, and 841 in the darker sections of fur and 739 and 738 for the more yellow areas. For the lighter areas, use 648 under the chin and blend into 3866. Add any highlights with BLANC.

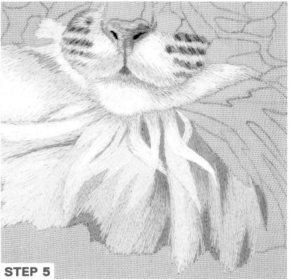

STEP 5

6 Using a lot of top shading, fill in the next portion of the neck fur with 3862, 3864, 738, 3866, 739, 3863, and 07.

7 Fill in the eyes with 844, 310, 3032, 3348, 648, 3364, 3013, and 613. Use 434 for the eyelid and 3861 with 452 for the inside edge of the eyelid.

tip **You can add a little highlight in the pupil of the eye by adding 3768 next to the eyeshine.**

STEP 6

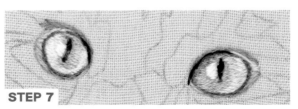

STEP 7

8 Stitch the left side of the face using 437, 438, 739, 3866, and 3863, using 436, 453, and 434 for the stripes. Do the same with the right side of the face. Add a few stitches of 3862 and 801 in the dark area below the tear duct.

STEP 8

tip **See Stripes and Speckled Fur (page 41), for directions on the method of stitching tabby stripes.**

9 Fill in the right side of the neck fur with 3864, 738, 739, 3866, 648, and BLANC. Continue working up the side of the face with 07, 738, 3864, 3863, 648, 739, and 842. Add a few top stitches of BLANC near the outer edge of the fur.

STEP 9

10 To make the ears, first stitch the outer edge of the ear with 3866 and 842. Use 8364 along the edge of the inside of the ear. Start filling in the inside of the ear with 452 and 453. Use 648, 02, 07, and BLANC to fill in the inner ear hairs, extending them out past the edge of the ear for a fluffy look. Do the same to the left ear.

STEP 10

11 Next, add 453 above the nose, and then blend into 435, 3863, 801, and 3862. Stitch around the nose with 437, 3864, and 3863.

12 Stitch the white area above the eye with 739 and BLANC. Use 801, 3846, 435, and 436 to stitch the forehead stripes. Fill in the fur between the stripes with 436, 437, 738, 3864, 3863, 3866, and 739.

Use the same method to fill in the right side of the forehead. Add a shadow on the right side of the nose's upper bridge, by the eye, by top shading in some 3864.

STEP 11

STEP 12

13 Add whiskers with BLANC and split stitches.

STEP 13

Golden Retriever | *Guinness*

BLONDE FUR CAN BE REALLY DIFFICULT since it can appear yellow, brown, or even green toned in the shadows. A profile portrait makes the subject look distinguished, as you'll see with Guinness. This pattern was stitched on white cotton twill.

Photo by Breanne Hodgson

Fur path guide

THREAD COLORS

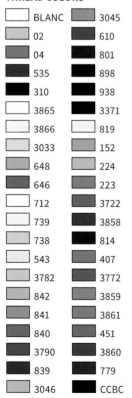

BLANC	3045
02	610
04	801
535	898
310	938
3865	3371
3866	819
3033	152
648	224
646	223
712	3722
739	3858
738	814
543	407
3782	3772
842	3859
841	3861
840	451
3790	3860
839	779
3046	CCBC

Color guide

EMBROIDERY

1 Begin this portrait by stitching the collar. Use 610, 3045, and 3046 to make the bronze buckle. Use 3371 for the holes and then use 898, 938, and 801 to fill in the leather collar.

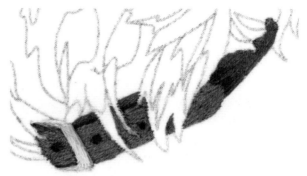

STEP 1

2 Starting with the shadow under the chin, use 648, 646, 3782, 3033, and 3866 to stitch the left edge of the neck. Add deeper shadows with 3790. Keep filling in the next section of the neck with 739, 712, 543, 3866, 3033, 3782, and 738. Use 3865 and top stitching to add some highlights on the fur.

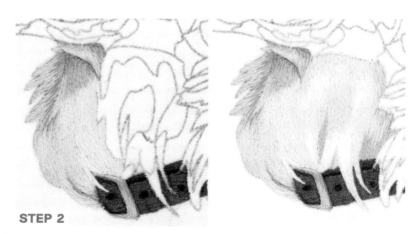

STEP 2

3 Finish the lower half of the neck by stitching the fur by the ear with 3866, 739, 842, 3033, 646, and 3782.

STEP 3

4 Fill in the nose holes with 310 and then stitch the nose with 3772, 407, 224, 451, and 3860. Add a few highlights with 819.

tip **See Noses in Profile View (page 46) for more detailed directions for stitching a dog nose in profile.**

STEP 4

5 Next, move on to the mouth. Use short and precise stitches here. Start on the tongue with 223, 3722, 3858, and 814. Fill in the teeth and gums with 224, 152, 3859, 3858, 223, 779, and 3861. Use 3782 and 3866 to stitch the teeth. Add a small shadow to the bottom canine with 842. Outline the edge of the tongue before filling it in to create a crisp line.

Stitch the gums on the edge of the mouth by using CCBC, 310, 779, 3861, 535, and 152. Add some highlights to the lip with 318 and use 819 to add some small highlights to the tongue to make it look wet.

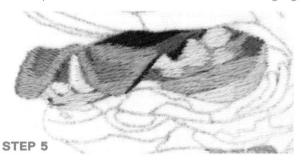 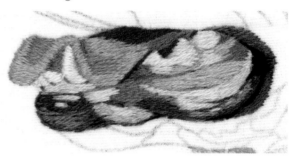

STEP 5

6 Fill in the lower part of the chin with 646, 779, 3790, 3782, and 3033.

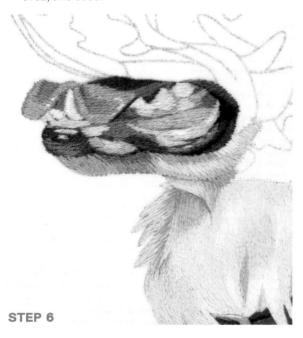

STEP 6

7 Starting at the nose, begin filling in the snout. Use CCBC and 535 near the nose. For the pink tones in the snout, stitch a layer of 779 and 451, and then use 535, 648, and 04 to stitch small hairs on top of it. Fill in the inside of the lip with 310 and then the outer edge of the lip in the background with 779 and 535. Continue filling in the snout with BLANC, 02, and 648.

STEP 7

8 Fill in the top of the snout with 840, 841, 3782, and 842. Then work downward with 739, 3866, and 3033.

STEP 8

9 Using small stitches, fill in the eye with 310, 938, 535, and 839; add a highlight with BLANC. Use 535, 779, 3782, and 04 to stitch the area around the eye. Add small eyelashes with 3033. Make a fur ridge with 3790 and 648 near the edge of the eye.

tip **See Eyes in Profile View (page 48) for a closer look at stitching an eye in profile.**

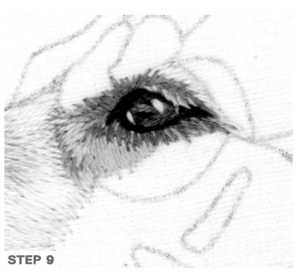

STEP 9

10 Fill in the top of the head with 3866, 3782, 3033, 842, and 648. Add some small hairs to the eyebrow with 841. Use 02 and 04 to add some small gray hairs near the eye. For the yellow patch on the temple, stitch a layer of 739 and use top shading to add a slight shadow of 842.

11 Continue filling in the side of the face with 3033, 841, and 842. Use 3033 and 648 for the shadow of the cheekbones and blend into 3866. Use top stitching to add a highlight with BLANC. For the lower part of the cheek, use 3033, 3866, 3865, and 3790, and blend into the neck with 543. Add a highlight with 3865.

STEP 10

STEP 11

12 Begin stitching the ear by using 3033, 739, 3782, 3866, 841, 842, and 646. Use 840 to deepen the cracks of fur in the ear.

STEP 12

13 Starting at the top and working downward, fill in the upper portion of the ear with 648, 3033, 739, and 3790.

STEP 13

14 Finish the ear using 648, 3790, 840, 3782, 3866, 3033, and 842. Add highlights to the ear fur with 3866.

STEP 14

Corgi | *Kenzie*

DON'T FORGET TO ADD A BIT OF SKIN TONE NEAR THE EAR CANAL WHEN STITCHING THESE PERKY EARS.

There is less fur near the center of the ear, so the skin shows through. This pattern was stitched on Kona Cotton in the color Shale.

Photo by Henry Montgomery and Charlie Nunn Photography

Fur path guide

THREAD COLORS

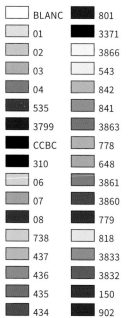

BLANC	801
01	3371
02	3866
03	543
04	842
535	841
3799	3863
CCBC	778
310	648
06	3861
07	3860
08	779
738	818
437	3833
436	3832
435	150
434	902
433	

Color guide

EMBROIDERY

1 Start at the top of the head near the ear. Use 801 for the shadow and then blend upward with 435, 434, 436, and 738.

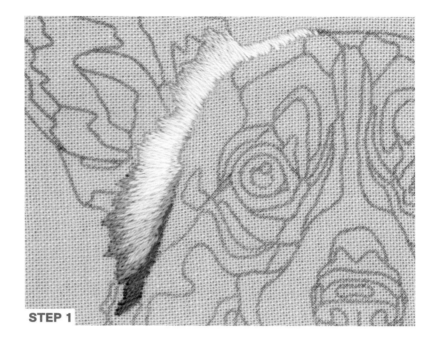

STEP 1

2 For the left ear, begin by stitching the outer edge with 436 and 07. Top shade with 840 at the base near the top of the head. Fill in the lower area of the ear with 779, 435, 436, and 06. For the larger portion of the ear, stitch the pink area with 778. Use top shading with 3861 and 3860. Deepen the pink area of the ear with 779.

Stitch a layer of 648 in the remaining area of the ear, and then make sparse stitches with 07 to add some darker hairs. Fill in the section of the ear near the edge with 07 and 08. Use 08 to make a few stitches in the ear fur for cracks in the fur.

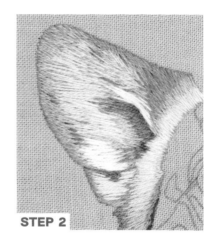

STEP 2

3 Using the same colors and technique as the previous step, complete the right ear.

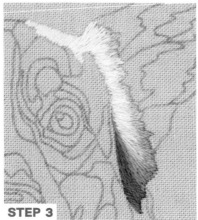

STEP 3

4 Before starting the face, fill in the eyes. Use 310, 433, 435, and BLANC. In the corner of the eyes add 03. Add small highlights along the eyelid with 04.

STEP 4

5 Continue filling in the face by stitching the forehead. Use 435, 648, and 3866 to stitch the eyebrow area. Add small darker hairs with 535. Keep filling in the forehead and brow with 738, 435, 437, and 436. For the lighter spot next to the eye, use 648 and a few small stitches of 535. Use 3371 to extend the edge of the eye outward.

6 Next, move to stitching the area under the eye. Blend the black eyelid into the fur with 3371. Use 435, 738, and 437 to create the shadows and highlights.

STEP 5

STEP 6

7 Using the same colors, follow the color guide and fill in the right side of the face. Add some small eye shines to the pupil with 535.

STEP 7

8 Fill in the nose with 310, CCBC, 3799, and 535. Add highlights with 04 and 03. Use 01 to stitch the small shadow of fur around the edge of the snout.

STEP 8

9 Using BLANC, fill in the middle of the snout and make the white streak going up the forehead. Use 535, 02, and 03 to add the area of dark fur above the nose and under the nose.

STEP 9

10 Use 902, 150, 3832, and 3833 to stitch the tongue. Add small highlights with 818. Continue stitching the rest of the mouth with 3799 and 310. Use 01 for the teeth and add a small shine on the lip with 02.

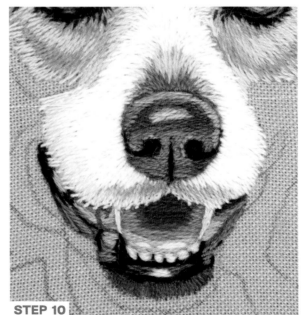

STEP 10

11 Start filling in the left side of the face. Use 08, 433, 3863, 437, and 842 near the side of the mouth. Blend the side of the face into the orange fur with 3866, 543, 437, and 738. Add a highlight on the cheek with BLANC.

12 Stitch the chin with 3799 and BLANC, and add a few chin hairs with 03 and top stitching. Use 841, 842, and 543 for the shadow under the chin, and then blend out to the left with 3866 and BLANC.

STEP 11

STEP 12

13 Fill in the area to the right of the mouth with 3866, 3799, 08, and 3863. Finish the right side of the neck fur with 543, 436, 3866, 842, 437, BLANC, 435, and 434.

14 Complete the portrait by stitching small whiskers around the mouth with 04.

STEP 13

STEP 14

Tabby Cat | *Pepper*

TABBY CAT FUR CAN BE REALLY DIFFICULT. There will be a lot of layering and top stitching to create the speckled fur. Some brown tabbies have a green/gray undertone to their fur, which you can capture by stitching a layer of color and then adding a blend of other colors on top of it. This pattern was stitched on white cotton twill.

Fur path guide

THREAD COLORS

	BLANC		3863
	01		3862
	02		938
	03		3371
	04		452
	535		3861
	CCBC		3779
	310		3859
	648		407
	646		632
	844		779
	07		772
	3033		372
	842		3364
	841		520
	839		931
	3790		

Color guide

EMBROIDERY

1 Begin this portrait by stitching the eyes and nose. Use 310, 844, 3364, 372, 520, 931, and 772 for the eyes. Fill in the nose with 310, 779, 3859, 3779, and 632.

tip **For a more detailed guide to stitching the eyes and nose of this cat, see Thread Painting Facial Features (page 45).**

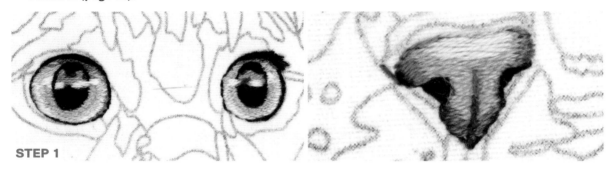

STEP 1

2 Next, move to the chin. Fill in the dark area of the lips with CCBC, and continue filling in the chin with 452, 01, BLANC, 02, 04, 03, and 648. Use 535 to stitch a few hairs near the top of the lip.

3 Fill in the left cheek with 03 and 04 near the center and bottom of the mouth, and make the white area with BLANC. Use a blend of 535, 648, and 07 near the top of the cheek. Make the whisker area with 842, 841, and 535. Add the darker spots of the whisker area with CCBC. Do the same to the right side of the cheek.

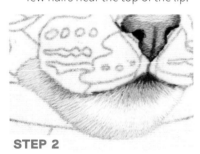

STEP 2

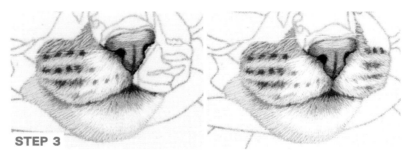

STEP 3

4 Begin stitching the area under the eye. For the lighter area, use 535, 3863, 842, 01, and 3033. Make the tabby stripes with 844, CCBC, and 3371. For the tabby fur, use a blend of 646, 648, 535, and 01.

tip **See Stripes and Speckled Fur (page 41) for a longer explanation on blending tabby fur and stripes.**

5 Finish filling in the left side of the face with 844, 535, 3790, 646, and 648.

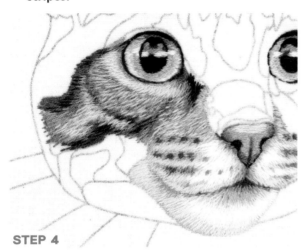

STEP 4

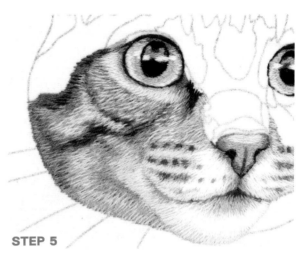

STEP 5

6 Using the same colors and technique, fill in the right side of the face. Add 841 near the chin.

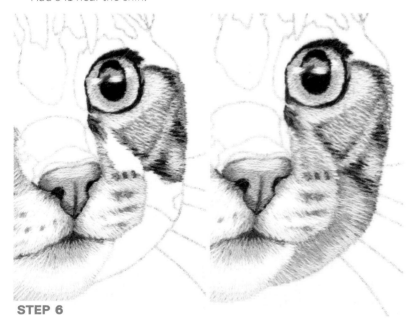

STEP 6

7 Move to the bridge of the nose and fill it in with CCBC, 938, 839, 3862, and 841. Make the spots to the left of the nose with CCBC.

STEP 7

8 Work upwards and fill in the center of the face. For the lighter areas near the eyes, use 842, 01, and 3863. Use 646, 648, 535, and 3790 to fill in the face between the eyes.

STEP 8

9 Fill in the forehead stripes with 844, 535, and 3371. Use 535, 648, and 646 to fill in the forehead between the stripes, and then add 01 to the lighter areas.

STEP 9

10 Moving to the right side of forehead, use 535, 646, 04, and 648 and fill in the remaining area.

STEP 10

11 For the left side of the forehead, use 646, 648, and 535. For the stripes and dark area near the ear, use 844, 535, and 3371.

12 Outline the left ear with 839, 841, 646, 535, and 648. Fill in the outer side of the ear with 3861, 407, CCBC, 07, 632, 452, and 648. For the inner area of the ear, blend together 07 and 407. Use 452 and 3861 to finish filling in the inside of the ear.

13 For the hairs inside the ear, use 839 near the inner edge, and then blend out with 07, 646, 535, and 01.

STEP 11

STEP 12

STEP 13

14 Using the same technique and colors of the left ear, fill in the right ear.

STEP 14

15 To finish the portrait, stitch the whiskers using a split stitch in BLANC.

STEP 15

Maltese Mix | *Forrest*

ALTHOUGH IT'S TEMPTING TO USE LONG STITCHES IN AREAS OF LONG FUR, using them exclusively makes the embroidery look unrealistic. Use longer stitches sparingly to represent longer fur, but make sure to blend it in with shorter stitches. This pattern was stitched on off-white cotton twill.

Photo by Roxanne Lacanilao

Fur path guide

THREAD COLORS

☐ BLANC		☐ 3033	
☐ 01		☐ 648	
☐ 02		☐ 646	
☐ 03		☐ 3866	
☐ 04		☐ 842	
☐ 535		☐ 841	
☐ 3799		☐ 840	
☐ CCBC		☐ 839	
☐ 310		☐ 838	
☐ 543		☐ 06	
☐ 3864		☐ 07	
☐ 3863		☐ 08	
☐ 3862			

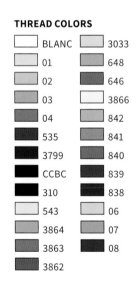

Color guide

EMBROIDERY

1 Starting with the left ear, work from darkest to lightest in each section. Fill in the ear with 07, 08, 838, 3863, 839, 840, 3862, 3864, 841, and 543.

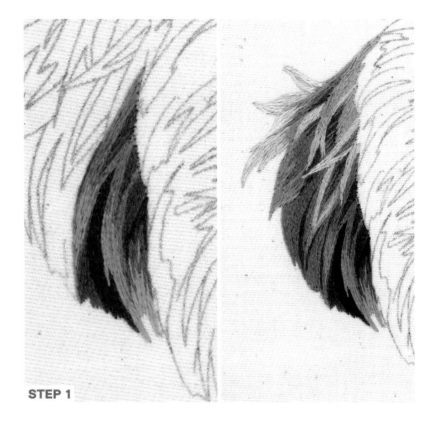

STEP 1

2 Using the same method and colors as the left ear, fill in the right ear.

tip **Stitching long fur is all about working from the background to the foreground. Break hairs down into sections and work on them individually. Keep your stitches a shorter length and don't make them too long or the embroidery can look messy.**

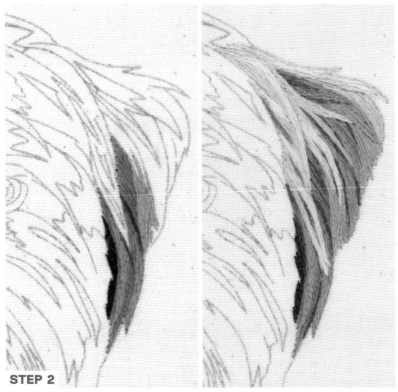

STEP 2

3 Move down to the chin. First, fill in the chin with 648, 06, 3866, and 842. Use 646 in the cracks of the fur near the mouth and in the chin hair. Fill in the lower lip with 310, 3799, 535, and 04, and add a small highlight with 03. Leave space for the hairs that fall in front of the lip. Stitch small hairs under the bottom lip with 648, 3033, and BLANC.

STEP 3

4 Outline the eyes with 310. Use 3799 to fill in the pupil. Add a highlight with 03, and fill in the rest of the eye with CCBC. Use 04 and 03 to add a small highlight along the lower eyelid.

tip **Some dog eyes don't have a visible black pupil in photos. Highlight instead with gray.**

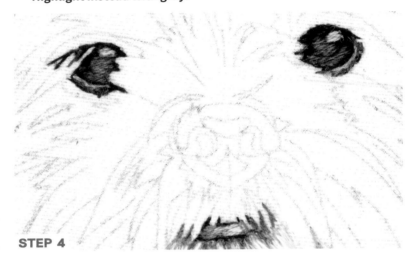

STEP 4

5 Stitch the long eyelash hair on top of the eye with 3864, 3863, and 839. Fill in the area under the eye and along the side of the face with 838, 840, 841, 3863, 543, 3864, 06, and 07.

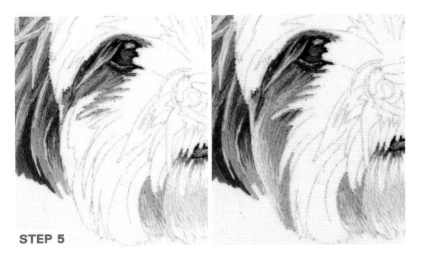

STEP 5

6 Starting around the eye, fill in the right side of the face with 838, 840, 3864, 3863, 543, 3866, and 842.

STEP 6

7 Fill in the left eyebrow with 839, 3863, 842, 840, and 08.

STEP 7

8 Continue up the left side of the head with 543, 3863, and 3864.

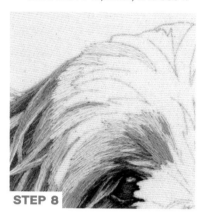

STEP 8

9 Fill in the right eyebrow with 3863, 839, 840, 841, 838, 842, and 543.

STEP 9

10 Moving around the right side of the head, use 543, 842, 3862, and 06 to fill in the hair near the edge of the face.

STEP 10

11 Use 01, 3866, and 543 to create the darker areas of the fur; use BLANC to fill in the rest of the fur on the forehead. To stitch the area between the eyes, use 648 and 3866 and blend into the forehead.

STEP 11

12 Fill in the nose with 310, 3799, 535, 04, and 03. Add small hairs in front of the nose with 01.

STEP 12

13 Work in layers for the mustache area. Stitch the darkest cracks in the fur first to use as guidelines, and fill in between them and build up to the lighter colors. For the shadows between the fur, use 310, 3799, and 535. Stitch some lighter hairs with 04, 638, 03, and 02. Add small highlights with 01 and BLANC.

STEP 13

14 Fill in the area above the nose with 3866, 3864, and BLANC. Make sure the fur extends to in front of the eyes.

STEP 14

15 For the remaining left side of the face, use 01, BLANC, 3033, 842, and 648.

STEP 15

16 Complete the portrait by filling in the right side of the face with BLANC, 3866, 842, and 06.

STEP 16

Poodle Mix | *Jude*

CURLY FUR CAN BE QUITE OVERWHELMING AT FIRST, but you can break it down into manageable sections. Work from the back to the front (meaning stitch the darker areas first and work your way to the foreground with lighter colors) and follow the stitch-direction guidelines. For a guide on stitching curls and waves, see Thread Painting Curves and Curls (page 40). The poodle pattern is quite possibly the most challenging one in the book, so take it slow and work on it curl by curl. This pattern was stitched on off-white cotton twill.

Photo by Stacy Dubuc

Fur path guide

THREAD COLORS

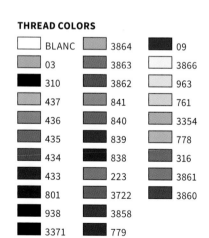

BLANC	3864	09
03	3863	3866
310	3862	963
437	841	761
436	840	3354
435	839	778
434	838	316
433	223	3861
801	3722	3860
938	3858	
3371	779	

Color guide

EMBROIDERY

1 Begin stitching the neck near the chin, and work your way outward toward the shoulders. Use 3371, 938, and 801 to create the fur here. Create subtle highlights by top stitching with 433.

This portrait can be a bit complicated to follow. The colors for the shadows and highlights in the fur can be broken down as follows:

Shadows: 3371, 938, 801, 838, 839

Mid tones: 435, 434, 433, 3863, 3862, 840

Highlights: 436 437, 3864, 841

STEP 1

2 Moving to the left ear, start at the top and work your way downward. Work from the back to the front, stitching the shadows first and then layering up to the highlights. Use 3371, 938, 801, 433, 435, 3864, 3863, 3862, and 434 for this section.

tip **See Thread Painting Curves and Curls (page 40) to learn how to stitch waves and curls.**

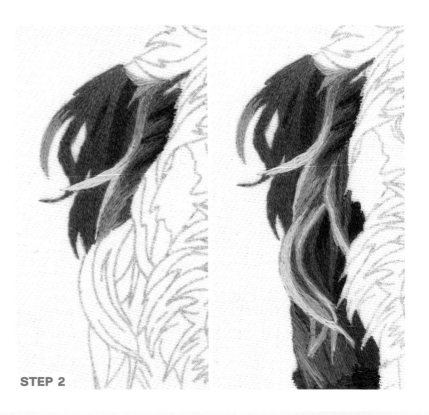

STEP 2

3 Using the same colors in the previous step, fill in the right ear.

STEP 3

4 Moving to the mouth, first stitch in the chin with 938, 801, and 3371. Next, fill in the gums with 3858, 3722, 223, 09, and 778, and the teeth with 3866. Finish the mouth by stitching the tongue with 3861, 778, 3354, and 963. Use top blending with 316 and 761. See Thread Painting Facial Features (page 45) for a step-by-step guide.

5 Stitch the eyes before filling in the face. Use 310, 938, 801, 434, and 435 to create each eye. Highlight the pupils with 03 and BLANC.

STEP 4

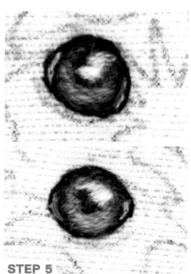

STEP 5

6 Stitch the eyebrow and under-eye area on both sides of the face. On the left side, use 3371, 838, 801, and 3862 under the eye. Use 3371, 801, 840, 839, 3864, and 3962 above the eye. On the right side, use 3371, 838, 801, 840, and 3862 under the eye. Use 3371, 801, 839, 840, 3864, 3863, 838, 434, and 938 above the eye.

7 For the nose, use 3371, 3858, 779, 09, 3860, and 3861. See Thread Painting Facial Features (page 45) for a guide on the nose.

STEP 6

STEP 7

8 Start filling in the snout under and around the nose. Continue working from shadows to highlights. Use 3371, 938, 801, 433, 3862, and 839 in this section. Stitch the darkest cracks in the fur first to use as guidelines, and fill in between them with the lighter colors. Work from the nose outward.

9 For the right side of the snout, use 938, 801, 3862, 3863, 435, 3864, 436, and 839.

STEP 8

STEP 9

10 Keep filling in the snout by using 838, 3862, 3863, 436, and 839 and working your way up to the forehead.

STEP 10

11 Stitch the area between the eyes with 3862, 436, 3864, 838, 433, 801, and 840.

STEP 11

12 Fill in the left side of the forehead with 3862, 839, 801, 838, and 3863.

STEP 12

13 Complete the portrait by filling in the right side of the forehead. Use 3371, 801, 3864, 3862, 3863, 839, 838, and 801 for this area.

STEP 13

ACCENTING PET PORTRAITS

There are many ways to add accents to pet portraits. You can add a flower crown, a collar, a border, some simple vines going up the side, a banner with the pet's name, or all of the above!

FLORAL ACCENTS

Lots of different types of flowers can be made with only a few stitches. Follow the provided patterns (page 134) or draw out your own. Mix and match and come up with your own designs!

Simple Daisy

Make a simple daisy by making backstitches with 2 strands of thread from the outside of your petals toward the center. Build up the stitches until the petals are filled in. Add French knots (page 129) to the center.

Heart Flower

Use a backstitch and 2 strands of thread to fill in each of the heart-shaped petals. Use 2 different colors of French knots to complete the center of the flower. Add an accent by stitching in a darker color on the lower half of the petals.

tip **Backstitch guidelines to follow so your petals have a curve to them.**

Easy Leaves

Split the leaf down the center and, using diagonal backstitches, fill in one-half. Fill in the second half, stitching from the outside to the inside so the stitches meet in the center.

For a fuller leaf, split it in half with a long stitch and then angle stitches from the top down to the bottom of the leaf.

Make leaves look fancy by adding extra stitches down the center.

Woven Roses

To start a woven rose, first draw a circle and split it into fifths. Using all 6 strands of thread, make a single long backstitch on each of the inner guidelines. These are the spokes you will weave over and under to create the rose. Stitch each spoke going from the outside ring to meet in the center.

Bring your needle up through the fabric next to the center, and then, skipping a spoke, weave it under the next one, making sure you don't poke through the fabric. Weave the needle over and under every other spoke until you've filled in the rose. Go in a counterclockwise direction, turning the hoop if you need to get a better angle. Work slowly and don't pull the thread so tight that the rose is warped. Make sure none of the spokes are sticking out at the end. You can do some stem stitches around the outside of the rose to cover them if needed. To end the rose, take your needle back down through the fabric just on the outside next to the rose and tie it off behind the hoop.

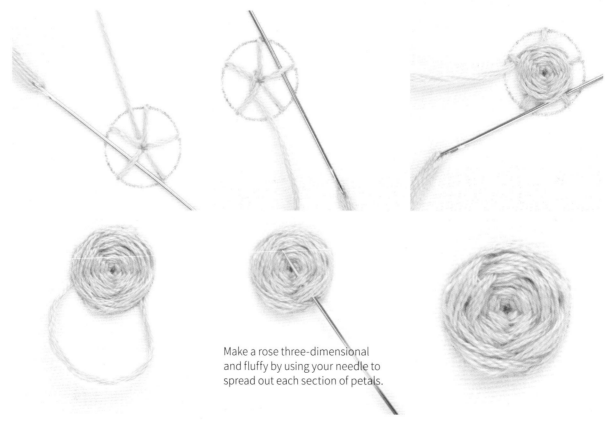

Make a rose three-dimensional and fluffy by using your needle to spread out each section of petals.

Add more detail to the roses by making them 2 colors or of variegated thread, or by adding French knots to the center.

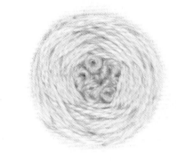 

French Knots

French knots make a great filler for floral elements. Use them to stitch the center of flowers, to create lavender, or to fill in areas between larger flowers and leaves.

To create a French knot, use 2 strands of thread. Bring the needle up through the fabric and then wrap the thread around the shaft of the needle 2–4 times. Poke the needle back down into the fabric just next to where you originally came up. Still holding the working thread, slide the thread wrapped around the needle to rest on top of the fabric. Then pull the needle through to lock the French knot in place.

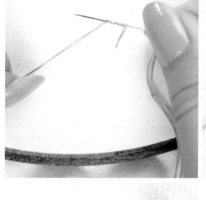 

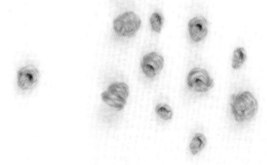

The more times you wrap the thread around the needle, the larger and taller the French knot will be.

tip **To prevent any trouble with pulling the needle through the fabric, use a needle with an eye that is the same width as the rest of the needle.**

GARLANDS

An easy way to accent a portrait is by adding symmetrical vines. Garland patterns can be found in Patterns (page 134). Stitch the leaves first, working from the tip of the leaf to the base, making sure to angle your stitches to come to a point where your leaf meets the vine. Make the centerline of the vine with a stem stitch. Vines can be all one color, the stem can be a darker or lighter color, or you can use a gradient going from top to bottom.

BANNERS

Banners are a fun way to accent the pet's name in the portrait. Banner patterns are in Patterns (page 134). Use either a stem stitch or a split backstitch to create the banner. Add the pet's name in the banner by using the alphabets also in Patterns.

LETTERS

Make your portrait more personalized by adding the pet's name.

Use your own handwriting or the letter patterns to create the name. Use small split backstitches. If a stitch isn't in the correct position, you can use couching to put it in place.

For cursive letters, use small stitches when creating the curves in the letters. The other print type can either be a serif or sans serif font.

tip **Before writing out the letters, draw a straight line as a guide for them to sit on. This will make sure the text is straight.**

Photo by Tristan Gallagher

FINISHING EMBROIDERY HOOPS

There are multiple ways to finish the backs of hoops, but I suggest only using ways that use thread and not any sort of glue.

Trim the outer fabric down to about 1″ (2.5cm) around the hoop. Before doing this, make sure your embroidery is centered in the hoop and the fabric is pulled taut and that there are no wrinkles. Using 2 strands of thread, weave your needle in and out of the fabric around the outside of the hoop. This is called a *running stitch*. Do this along the outside edge of the fabric. Pull tight at the end to cinch in the fabric. Tie off the thread to secure. You can leave the back open or cover it with another piece of fabric or felt.

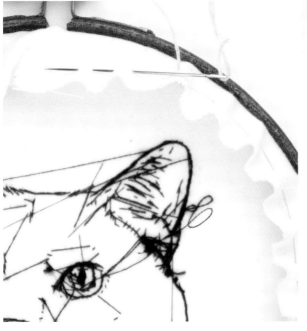

To add backing to a hoop, cut a circle of fabric or felt to cover the back and secure it to the back of the hoop by bringing your needle through both the edge of the backing material and the embroidery fabric. When cutting the circle shape, use the outside edge of the inner embroidery hoop as your guide.

You can also frame your portraits in decorative frames.

Display your artwork by hanging it on a wall or by placing it on a shelf, bookcase, or table.

Photo by Tristan Gallagher

CONCLUSION

Photos by Estefany Gonzalez

2014 versus 2020

I know I covered a lot in this book and that it can all seem pretty overwhelming, but I promise you can do it.

Don't stress about getting every detail perfect; focus on capturing the overall idea and the look and feel of the portrait. You will get better in time. The more you practice the better you will become!

I've always known that skill is something you have to develop over time. My pet portrait embroideries didn't always look like they do now. You have to try and grow and that sometimes comes with some failure in between. I believe this is something everyone can do, and I can't wait to see where your thread painting journey takes you.

The most important thing is to stay curious about your art. Striving to discover something new to you is a surefire way to grow and make embroideries that are uniquely your own. You've made your start, and over time you'll realize the results of your effort!

PATTERNS

Downloadable Patterns

Full-size downloads of the patterns are available at:

tinyurl.com/11414-patterns-download

Accessing patterns

- To access the pattern through the tiny url, type the web address provided into your browser window.

- To access the pattern through the QR code, open the camera app on your phone, aim the camera at the QR code, and click the link that pops up on the screen.

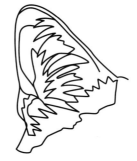

Enlarge 200%.

Enlarge 200%.

Enlarge 200%.

Aa Bb Cc Dd Ee Ff
Gg Hh Ii Jj Kk Ll
Mm Nn Oo Pp Qq
Rr Ss Tt Uu Vv Ww
Xx Yy Zz

Aa Bb Cc Dd Ee Ff
Gg Hh Ii Jj Kk Ll
Mm Nn Oo Pp Qq
Rr Ss Tt Uu Vv Ww
Xx Yy Zz

1 2 3 4 5 6 7 8 9 0
( ) + / - & ? !

SUPPLIES AND RESOURCES

Here are some useful links that will help you on your own embroidery journey.

SUPPLIES

Thread

DMC
dmc.com

Fabric

Kona Cotton
robertkaufman.com > from the *Select collection:* drop-down menu, click Kona Cotton

Needles

John James Needles
jjneedles.com

Embroidery Hoops

Frank A. Edmunds Co.
faedmunds.com > Products > Embroidery

ADDITIONAL RESOURCES

Thread color conversion chart
cyberstitchers.com > Stitching Tools > Floss Conversion Charts

Classic Colorworks
classiccolorworks.com

Gütermann thread
123stitch.com > search Gütermann

Sulky Fabri-Solvy Stabilizer
sulky.com

Wacom
wacom.com

DMC thread color palettes
stitchpalettes.com

ABOUT THE AUTHOR

MICHELLE STAUB IS A SELF-TAUGHT EMBROIDERY ARTIST WHO HAS BEEN CREATING PET EMBROIDERIES SINCE 2014. SHE LOVES USING NEEDLE AND THREAD TO CREATE GORGEOUS KEEPSAKES.

An Ohio native, Michelle lives with her husband, dog, and three cats who provide her with equal parts inspiration and frustration. Her pet portraits have been featured in magazines, on television, and on websites around the world. You can find all of her work on Instagram and on her website.

Use the tag **#modernthreadpainting** to share embroidery made with this book or your very own pet portraits!

Visit Michelle online and follow on social media!

Website: stitchingsabbatical.com

Facebook: /stitchingsabbatical

Instagram: @stitchingsabbatical

YouTube: /stitchingsabbatical